WHY YOU SHOULD GIVE A DAMN ABOUT ECONOMICS

WHY YOU SHOULD GIVE A DAMN ABOUT ECONOMICS
The US Debt Crisis and Your Future

LESLIE A. RUBIN

BROWN BOOKS
PUBLISHING GROUP

Why You Should Give a Damn About Economics
The US Debt Crisis and Your Future

Brown Books Publishing Group
Dallas, TX / New York, NY
www.BrownBooks.com
(972) 381-0009

A New Era in Publishing®

Publisher's Cataloging-In-Publication Data

Names: Rubin, Leslie A., author.
Title: Why you should give a damn about economics : the US debt crisis and your future
    / Leslie A. Rubin.
Description: Dallas, TX ; New York, NY : Brown Books Publishing Group, [2024] |
    Includes bibliographical references.
Identifiers: ISBN: 978-1-61254-646-9 | LCCN: 2023951473
Subjects: LCSH: Debts, Public--United States--History--21st century. | Financial crises-
    -United States-- History--21st century. | United States--Economic conditions. |
    United States--Politics and government. | Macroeconomics. | BISAC: BUSINESS &
    ECONOMICS / Economics / Macroeconomics. | BUSINESS & ECONOMICS /
    Government & Business. | BUSINESS & ECONOMICS / Economics / Theory.
Classification: LCC: HJ8101 .R83 2024 | DDC: 336.340973--dc23

ISBN 978-1-61254-646-9
LCCN 2023951473

Printed in United States
10 9 8 7 6 5 4 3 2 1

For more information or to contact the author, please go to
www.MainStreetEconomics.com.

This book is dedicated to my wonderful family; my wife, Nermine; and my five children who have been supportive and tolerant of my occasional rantings about what is happening to this country. I must also acknowledge my parents, Myer and Lakie Rubin, may they rest in peace, who guided me and instilled in me a sense of fairness and humility. My thoughts about them inspire me every day.

CONTENTS

Part Two: Review of Our Major Issues

Foreword

This book was written out of a concern for the economic direction our country is going—to help you, the voter, understand our problems and to help our country choose a fiscally sustainable economic path forward.

Les Rubin cares about his country. He has had a successful career in real estate for fifty years, but today sees the fiscal situation in our country simply falling apart. The political conversations around our problems seem only to make matters worse. If you feel the same and share those concerns but want simple solutions that work for everyone, then this book is for you.

It's not too late to turn things around—yet!—but we can't wait for others to come to our rescue. It's our country and our lives we are talking about. The best thing we can do is educate ourselves on the basic issues and learn the basic economic concepts that will help get us out of this mess.

That is Les's belief. He had the benefit of traditional economics classes as a college student and, more importantly, has had a lifetime of experience applying them since the mid-1960s. He believes in sharing his experience and insights with you, me, and everyone he can so we can understand the issues and make our own decisions, ask our politicians for better solutions, and even elect better politicians who will deal with the problems, if those in Congress now will not. It's still we the people in control, but we can only drive if we know where we want to go.

Economic mismanagement has consequences for business, for personal life and for our country. If you spend more than you than you earn, you eventually get crushed by debt and go bankrupt. In business, you eventually close shop. The same is true for countries. Overburdened by debt, they fall into crisis and can even collapse. We don't want that for ourselves or our children, but it's sadly moving in that direction already.

US government spending is totally out of control. Neither party seems to care and debt is piling up even faster than what gets reported in the press. That's where actually understanding the problem matters.

We hear in the press about our current debt which is just what we have officially issued today. That's already at an all-time high of $32+ trillion and growing rapidly, already larger than the size of the entire US economy. It hasn't been that large (as a percentage of the overall economy) since we had to finance WWII.

But that doesn't begin to capture the real problem. The US Treasury Department explained in its own executive summary in 2022 that the "current fiscal path is unsustainable."[1] On September 30, 2022, in financial statements published by the Department of the Treasury, they explained that our total financial obligations are actually $122 trillion. $122 *trillion* dollars. Trillion. Let that sink in. That's *$122,000,000,000,000.*

And that means $369,000 for every man, woman, and child. That's not "per household." That's you alone. That's me alone. That's what we are leaving for each of our kids. Do you have that? Does your spouse also have that? Does each of your kids have that? That is *our debt*.

Remember, it's *we* the *people*. It's our government and, in the end, we pay 100 percent of the bills of our government. It's *our debt*.

That ticking time bomb of debt is what set Les on a path to fix things. He believes that educating everyday, ordinary people in basic economics will lead to people voting better and will slowly put us back on the right path. He believes that it's all about knowing some basics and then applying common sense. He believes it's not a partisan issue. It's not right or left. We all need to understand these things and demand some changes. Les offers us all a solution: *learn economics* and *vote smart*. That's all. That's this book.

As an economics professor, I've been teaching economics now for over twenty years. When I met Les a few years ago, his enthusiasm was immediately contagious, and his mission resonated with me in my bones. As a lifelong teacher and student of economics, I can see the problem clearly. I too believe that a quality education and a lot of common sense can go a long way.

For a few years now, I've had the chance to read Les's weekly writings, providing him some feedback on topics and on the economic details. Les knows what he's talking about. He knows it as a businessperson. He knows it as a former CPA/controller. He knows it as a voter. But what impresses me most is that he knows it in his gut and has a talent for explaining it in everyday language that people want to hear. He boils down everything to its essence and makes it accessible to everyone. Hence the name of his foundation and blog: *Main Street Economics*.

This is the economics that people on Main Street need to understand. This is economics that works. It's survived the test of time and proven its worth. It's the economics you need to know in order to vote smart and save our country.

Les takes us on a journey. He explains why this stuff matters. He explains why we should care—or, as Les would say, "Why you should give a damn." He explains it in simple language because these are simple concepts, and everyone can understand them.

The book starts with an overview. In Part One he explains the economic system overall, all of the basic economic concepts you need to be familiar with, how different political choices matter for the system, and how all of that adds up for us to live better or worse lives. He walks us through supply and demand, how to use it to think about things, and what it all means. He reminds us why there are only a few fundamentals that are truly key like private property and the rule of law and how and why we should protect them.

Part Two applies basic economics and common sense to the issues that are most pressing. He focuses on the debt overall and its primary causes. He tackles the extremely thorny issue of entitlement reform. He explains slowly and simply what entitlements are, why we have them, and what they mean for every one of us. But after presenting the problems, he suggests reasonable reforms that would put us back on solid footing with the least pain for us all today. He moves from there to inflation, energy, and saving our planet. Again, all with solid, commonsense economic proposals that we can all understand and support.

I've been teaching in classrooms around the world for over twenty years. It's really exciting to see Les taking economics to the people. In the end, it's about you, the voter, the person living on Main Street making ends meet day to day. There's no one better to share his understanding and good sense with you and with us all.

LEARN ECONOMICS and VOTE SMART.

Thank you,

Chris Ball, PhD
István Széchenyi Chair in International Economics
Quinnipiac University

Acknowledgments

This book has been a labor of love for me. My concerns for the future of this country led me to want to provide some basic education on economics and communicate to the folks on Main Street the serious economic problems I see coming in the future.

But I am not an economist and realized I needed professionals to help me in this endeavor if this were to be a useful tool and guide in learning basic economics and explaining the issues that I believe are so important to us all. It had to be in plain, easy-to-understand language but technically correct.

I got that technical help from two professional economists, Tawni Hunt Ferrarini, PhD, and Howard J. Wall, PhD. Tawni is a longtime professor of economics, currently the Robert W. Plaster Professor of Economic Education at the Lindenwood University in St. Charles, Missouri, and is co-author of *Common Sense Economics*, which is in use in many countries around the world. Howard is Director at the Center for Applied Economics at Plaster College, Lindenwood University, in St. Charles, Missouri, and former vice president at the Federal Reserve Bank of St. Louis.

Without their prodding, encouragement, and technical support, this book would not have been completed. I thank them both for their expertise and support.

Not being an author, I had some fantastic help putting the manuscript in understandable language and form from Robyn Cohen, a professional writer and marketing advisor. The book would not have been the same without her expert advice.

After getting it drafted, I was introduced to Brown Books by a friend who had successfully published with them. One conversation with Milli

Brown was all it took. She was so excited and enthusiastic about what I was trying to do and in agreement with the issues I was addressing that I felt sure I had come to the right place. She explained the process to a novice like me—I was sold. That was a great decision. I did come to the right place.

The very capable staff improved the work greatly. I cannot be more thankful to have had their expert guidance. The Project Manager, Brittany Griffiths, who oversaw and coordinated the effort; Sterling Zuelch, who was the copy editor; and Carissa Demma, the line editor whose eagle eyes really refined and improved the work. We engaged an outside illustrator, Lisa Rothstein, who gave us some great cartoons to spice up the interest.

To all of them, I owe a great deal of thanks. Thank you.

AUTHOR'S NOTE

Most Americans are focused on the current issues they face every day, and the subject of economics is not high on their priority list. Most are busy with their daily activities in life, working, raising a family, getting the kids to their chosen sport to practice or play a game, or just enjoying life in a well-earned retirement.

But their economic well-being is very important to them, and that is a function of how well our economic system is managed. Whether they realize it or not, their economic interests today and into the future are dependent on various government policies and how they impact the economy. Sometimes the impact is as immediate as when inflation rears its ugly head or when we have an economic decline into a recession. Sometimes it is some intangible thing in the future, as might be the case if we harm our future economy with long-term governmental debts we cannot pay or follow policies which negatively impact our future economic well-being, perhaps by an economic decline in our real incomes and standard of living.

We inherited a country that worked well. It was formed by the brilliance of our Founding Fathers who sacrificed much and shed much blood to create the America we know. It has been fiercely protected through many wars and conflicts to survive as the greatest, strongest country in the world. And we owe it to our kids, grandkids, and all future generations to leave them with a country that still works well. We must be good stewards of this country. Are we doing that? Will future generations have the same opportunity that we have had? I fear not, and that is the primary reason for this book and why Main Street Economics Inc. was founded.

Many of our citizens have not had an opportunity to study the fundamentals of economics and may not grasp the importance of various policies promoted by our politicians and what they mean for today and the future. But the policies are quite important for their welfare today and in the future. Today, we are on an unlighted path into the future with policies and problems that could well lead to the economic destruction of America. We must grasp that reality before it is too late and take every action to be sure it does not happen.

Main Street Economics is a nonpartisan, nonprofit educational corporation which is devoted to making economics easy to understand and to alert, and even alarm, our citizens about the serious problems we are facing which will have very negative impacts on our future if we do not understand and correct them. While current economic policy is not an everyday concern, it is critical to the future of our country. The folks on Main Street, the "voting public," must understand the basics of economics and the implications of economic policy, so they can voice their opinions to our elected representatives, and if they will not listen, then voice their opinions in the voting booth.

I hope you will read and enjoy this book. Part One is basic economics for laymen, those who have not had a chance to study economics or a refresher for those have long forgotten about the fundamentals they learned long ago. It covers all of the important topics of Econ 101 in a brief, easy-to-read-and-understand overview. Part Two is focused on the most important problems we face and some ideas as to what can be done to be sure we fix our potential problems before they become fatal.

So relax, read, and enjoy your immersion in the "wonderful world of economics."

INTRODUCTION

When New York congresswoman Alexandria Ocasio-Cortez warned that the world would end in twelve years due to climate change, she fell short of noting the US national debt as another contributing factor. The federal government owes **$121,600,000,000,000**.[1] That's eleven zeros trailing off that six, making it in the *trillions*. And of the **$121.6 trillion**, **$32 trillion** is interest-bearing debt, and **$76 trillion** is unfunded liabilities of the federal government.[2] Those numbers are from the last financial report available from the government on September 30, 2022, and it's increased since then.[3]

Your share of it is **$368,000** . . . and climbing.

The **$121.6 trillion** debt on the collective government credit card is beyond comprehension, and the trends today will make it even worse in the future. The Congressional Budget Office (CBO), the government agency that makes nonpartisan estimations, projects large and growing deficits indefinitely based on current policy. And that's before some of the new, unpaid-for programs being proposed today. By 2033, the CBO projects the interest-bearing debt to grow by **$19.5 trillion**.[4] That will bring our interest-bearing part of the debt to over **$50 trillion**.[5]

The colossal debt owed by the federal government might eventually lead to the economy collapsing and mass starvation. Let that sink in. Economic instability has just as much of an impact on the food on your table as climate change. And not a lot of people are blowing their horns about economics like they are the environment.

I am not an economist; I am a businessman. I have been a real estate developer since the mid-1970s and was a CPA/controller for ten years before that. I've had success and failure multiple times. But after each failure, I managed to survive and, eventually, land on my feet and pay off all my debts. So why did I write a book on economics, public policy, and the problems we face?

I have watched our economic direction for years, but now I see a major problem coming as a result of our enormous debt. Even though I have only a fundamental education in economics from college, after a few years working in business, I realized that many folks never had, or nowadays get, a chance to learn about economics. So I learned more about it and got involved in economic education on a local basis. I became a founding member of the Pinellas Economic Development Corporation, served as the Chairman of the Pinellas Suncoast Chamber of Commerce, Founder of the Pinellas Economic Education Council, and was a key part of the team that made Enterprise Village, among many others—all to help the public learn about economics and know the risks and rewards that it entails.

To put it simply, I'm a deeply concerned citizen who cares about what is happening in our country. That's why I got involved in the beginning. That same reason is why I wrote this book.

My Purpose

Educate and inform—that's all I want to do. This book is written for those Main Street citizens, not students of economics, not teachers of it, and not those immersed in these subjects day in and day out. This book is for you—the voting public. It is meant to educate, not confound. Most people glaze over when they hear the term "economics" and walk away scratching their head saying, "What was that?" This book simplifies and teaches economics in a clear, logical way that you can understand and use in the real world.

I'm not here to promote any cause or political side. I do my best to keep things nonpartisan. Not Republican or Democrat. Not left or right. My only goal is to educate and alert people to the difficulties we face as well as which policies might best help solve these problems. I won't tell you how to vote, but I'll arm you with the facts so you can vote your conscience. A better-informed voting public allows you to vote intelligently for those who propose policies *you* favor and make good economic sense. So let's start our walk down the road of economics: what it is, how it works, and why you should care about any of this.

Why Should You Give a Damn?

The very future of our country, for you, your kids, and your grandkids, depends on the success of our economy. This will be determined by policies coming from our elected representatives, and it's the policies our public officials present that will propel our country toward, or away from, prosperity. Almost all policy proposals are made with good intentions and sound good on the surface. Unintended consequences frequently come back to bite us where the sun don't shine, but it is outcomes that matter, not intentions.

These officials will be elected by you. *You* and *your vote* will determine the future of this country: how well we live or what serious economic problems could bring us down. There are always many issues facing every country because nothing is ever perfect, but this is especially true for the United States today. We face some very daunting problems.

Throughout this book, I'll address many of these issues and how learning about economics will help you understand these issues, why they should be important to you, the welfare of future generations, and most importantly, what we should be doing about them. Part One examines the fundamental principles of economics—systems, supply and demand, the Federal Reserve System, and so many other factors in short, easy-to-understand language. Part Two explores and explains the most important modern problems we face today and includes recommendations to get our great nation back on track. Throughout the book, there will be Keep It Simple, Stupid Examples (or KISSE for short). These give brief examples, facts, or definitions that can help you remember the most crucial parts of economics. That's why I'm urging the voting public to take the time to learn and understand what is going on in the US today. With the way our world is right now—you need to understand economics more than ever before. Rich or poor, young or old . . . the decisions being made in DC affect us all.

So please, read on. I hope you will find this book informative and helpful.

Leslie A. Rubin

PART ONE
BASIC ECONOMICS FOR LAYMEN

"No, I don't really care about all that economics mumbo-jumbo. Why?"

CHAPTER 1

All About Economics

The Great Depression began in 1929 and ended around 1939. It is remembered as a time of mass unemployment with sharp increases in homelessness and poverty. If the United States continues its current debt trajectory, America will spiral into a nationwide depression much like we did almost a hundred years ago.

In fact, people are already gearing up for these so-called end-times by acquiring farmland and stocking up on food and rifles because they fear having to defend themselves down the road. A civilized economic system requires the ownership of private property and rule of law. If either is dismantled, an economic system of any kind is impossible.

Such a crash is expected to happen when the United States can no longer borrow any money. We're fortunate we're still able to, for now, but our debt is piling on—fast. And investors don't like to loan out money where they don't think they are going to be repaid.

What the Heck Is Economics Anyway?

Economics is the study of how businesses and individuals allocate (scarce) resources for production, distribution, and consumption—both individually and collectively. It affects your life every single day! Every time you go to the gas pump or shop for groceries, you experience what's going on with our economy. Feeling the pinch in your wallet? Living paycheck to paycheck? Wondering if you should only fill up half your tank now so it doesn't break your bank the next day? Having to find the cheapest gas station each time you need a fill-up? That's economics, and it's all impacted by our officials in Washington, DC.

In America, economics is all about how well people live and how free each person is to pursue happiness—so long as they don't harm or hurt others. This is all based on human nature. It is natural for all of us to make decisions that we think are in our best interest—it's basic psychology. Which brings us to the major areas of economic study: microeconomics and macroeconomics.

> **Microeconomics** focuses on the behavior of individual consumers and producers. **Macroeconomics**, on the other hand, examines overall economies on regional, national, or international scale.

Good economic policy can lead to prosperity throughout the nation. Bad economic policy can generate uncertainty in markets, put people out of jobs, raise prices, close businesses, and lead to major economic recessions/depressions. We don't always know what is really in our best interest, short-term or long-term. But we all want to live happily and improve our lives in a world of constraints. This involves "trade-offs"—doing more of this and less of that—and using our best judgment.

In the United States, we are fortunate to live under a system of government where we are free to make our own decisions and pursue what is in our best interest. We are allowed to work hard and be creative to gain benefits for ourselves and our family. Government policy, and how that affects our economic system, matters to the "free" and independent person because policies allow and restrict what can be done.

What Is an Economic System?

In each society, there's an order, or **economic system**, that makes the production, resource allocation, investment, and distribution run smoothly and continuously turns the economic wheel. **Command-directed economies** are decided at the top: the government owns the means of production and determines how scarce resources are allocated.

This is typical of a socialist form of government. **Demand-directed economies**, on the other hand, are governed by the people, who own the means of production and respond to what the consumers demand. These are also called **market economies**, since the market demand determines what is produced. Individually owned businesses try to earn a profit and must determine what is valued by consumers. Fulfilling this demand will determine what is produced and how scarce resources are allocated. There is relatively little government interference in day-to-day decisions of a **free enterprise**/market economic system.

There is a fundamental philosophical difference between command- and demand-directed economic systems. If you are an individual who wants to be free and "do your thing" and work hard to get ahead, then you will prefer some form of a demand economy. If you prefer for the government to direct what you do and provide for you as they think best, then you will prefer a command economy. We are all different and will do and vote for (if we can vote) what we think is best for us.

Neither command-directed or demand-directed economics operate in a pure form; there are many variations, and each is slightly different depending on where it lands on the command-versus demand-directed economy scale. As we will discuss in other chapters, the most prosperous countries have a free-enterprise/market system alongside government welfare or social programs to support people in different ways.

Which economic system is best? No one really agrees on this answer. Remember: opinions are like belly buttons—everyone has one! The big debate in the US right now is all about which is better for the country: free-enterprise/market economy or socialism. And to make a sound decision, you must understand what makes our economy work.

—$$$—

Do we own our life? Or does someone else own/control it? Most people think they own their life, and this ownership gives them the right to be free to pursue their own interest for their own sake and to keep the fruits of their labor. Economics provides the incentive, and when incentives are aligned properly with human nature, good things happen.

CHAPTER 2

Get to Know Economic Systems

You don't need to be a systems engineer to know systems. Really, it's all a bunch of parts assembled together, like a factory. There's a way of getting from point A to B and all the way to Z, and the checkpoints along the way keep it running smoothly. The same goes for economics: it needs a clean operation and a steady source of supplies to run efficiently. In this chapter, I'll discuss the four building blocks of an economy and how different economic systems (and what those are) use them.

The Building Blocks of an Economy

All economies function with the same basic building blocks, or resources, that date to caveman days. These resources are always present in some form to produce goods and services. They are consumed by people like you and me or used by businesses and producers to make different goods and services. Economic resources are said to be "scarce." That is, they are available in limited amounts. There are competing uses for them. So people allocate them to their various, competing uses. The four broad categories of resources are:

1. **Land.** Of course, land is needed for the production to take place. But land also refers to the raw materials used in production. To make steel, for example, we need land to put the steel mill on and raw materials (iron ore, carbon, oxygen, and fuel) to make the steel.

2. **Capital.** Buildings, equipment, computers, and other tangibles that are needed to produce goods and services are physical capital. There is also human capital like know-how and expertise and is closely linked to education and experience. Physical and human

11

capital are not money—financial capital is comprised of stocks, bonds, and loans that connect investors, borrowers, and lenders to make investments in capital possible.

3. **Labor.** This captures the time that people put into producing a physical product such as steel or providing a service such as banking. This includes direct labor, administration, and management.

4. **Entrepreneurship.** Entrepreneurship includes the creative and managerial parts of starting, owning, and running an operation for a firm that produces goods and services. It involves securing and organizing resources, strategic decision-making, and bearing the risks of ownership. An entrepreneur could be producing a new good, improving an existing service, discovering ways to reduce costs, or seizing profit opportunities that others have missed or not thought of.

In all economic systems, these four scarce resources are combined to create goods and services. What differs between the systems are the incentives, rules, and institutions that influence how these resources are allocated among their competing uses. The type of economic system put in place will determine who decides which goods are produced and in what quantities, how they are produced, who gets what produced, and at what price—all in using the available resources.

An In-Depth Look at Economic Systems

In the United States, we operate as a **demand** economy whereas the former Soviet Union was a **command** economy. Under the former Soviet Union's command economy, it was a bureau called the Central Planning Committee that determined what was produced. There was no pricing system to signal what people wanted. Instead, it was just the arbitrary whim of the controlling Central Planning Committee that determined production. Today, Russia is a mixed economy.

Let's explore how these systems work and how economies around the world tend to combine elements of both systems.

Market/Demand Economy

In 1776, Adam Smith, an economist and philosopher, viewed as the father of modern economics, published his treatise on economics: *An Inquiry into the Nature and Causes of the Wealth of Nations*. In this, Smith describes the workings of a market economy, where the natural inclinations of individuals motivate people to freely choose to help themselves by serving others in purposeful ways. As if guided by an "invisible hand," people in a market economy will constantly move to improve their households and businesses in mutually beneficial ways.

> "Every individual necessarily labors to render the annual revenue of society as great as he can. He generally neither intends to promote the public interest, nor knows how much he is promoting it. He intends only his own gain, and he is, in this, as in many other cases, led by an invisible hand to promote an end which was not part of his intention."
>
> —ADAM SMITH[1]

Smith means that it is human nature to want to do well and succeed for you, your family, and the other people who mean something to you. The "invisible hand" of self-interest leads to spontaneous "self-regulation" of the marketplace as individuals pursue their own interests and well-being by fulfilling the needs of others in the production of goods and services they value. There is no force. There is no exploitation. There is only cooperation and harmonious action and interaction. The unintentional consequence of these pursuits of self-interest is a growing economy and lifting society to a higher standard of living, including the most marginalized communities. Wonderful inventions, innovations, and technological advancements spring up when individuals can pursue their interests.

The main characteristic of a market economy is that it's **private**. Individuals are free to choose how to use their time, talents, and treasures as they desire, and consumer consumption of products and services determines what gets produced. The means of production are privately owned and protected by the **rule of law** (more on this in Chapter 6). So long as the producers don't bring harm or hurt to others, they can produce whatever they desire using the available resources. The consumers are free to buy what they want whenever they want. We see this every day in the US (a demand-based economy). For example, the iPhone gets produced because more than 1.5 billion active users worldwide demand it (as of February 2023).[2] Economists of market economies focus on the four factors of resources and the efficiency of how they are mobilized by businesses to bring goods and services to consumers like you and millions of others in exactly the right quantities, just-in-time, and at acceptable prices.

In a market-based economy, both individuals and businesses respond to **price signals**. These signals help communicate what to produce, how much, for whom, and at what price. Consumers send price signals through their priorities, values, and preferences for goods and services by choosing to purchase—or not. Businesses then balance the price signals and behaviors of consumers against their costs of production and the competing uses of available resources. If there's an alignment between the prices, consumer wants, and the product a business has created, a transaction (i.e., the purchase of a good and/or service) is made freely. Consumers are free to purchase or not, and businesses are free to produce or not. In other words, people are free to choose, and businesses transact only when there is a willing buyer and seller at a given price—so everyone wins.

The long and short of it is that businesses must make a profit to be able to produce and employ workers, and they can only do so if they satisfy consumers at acceptable prices high enough to cover their costs and make a profit. If a market price covers production costs and some profit, businesses have the incentive to supply what consumers want or need. If prices do not cover costs, businesses supply something else or shut down.

Consumers have choices, but their income, time, and talent are limited. They will only buy what businesses produce when personal benefits of doing so are higher than the prices paid. People may pay money for personal enjoyment of a hobby, which has a feeling of being priceless, but always comes with a dollar sign. Entertainment, fitness, and some forms of education make consumers feel good, but this is often weighed against a price tag. If one gym charges $10 a month while another costs $30, a person may go to the cheaper gym if it services the needs that they want. They may go to the more expensive gym if it has more amenities that are more in line with their goals and wants, making it worth the price.

Consumers do this dance every time they go to the grocery store too. With products galore to pick from, people will take into consideration the quantity that they are getting, the quality of the product, how much they have to pay for it, and how much they want it before they take it to the register. They'll pick the one they feel will give them the best end of the deal.

When a market economy is competitive, wealth and prosperity are brought about by the spontaneous actions and interactions of millions of consumers and producers voluntarily responding to price signals. Prices are set by the intersection of supply and demand (which is explained in Chapter 3).

Government operates in a limited capacity for market economies. Government officials work in the background but are still instrumental. They provide services to citizens, protection of their freedoms and rights to person and property through evenhanded enforcements, and provision of a few public goods such as national defense. All these are key to letting incentives and market forces lift standards of living to new heights.

If government did not serve in this limited capacity and there were no protections of persons or property, then the brute with the biggest club would simply take what others have. Businesses would not invest if there were no protection of their investments. Consequently, market transactions would drop, production would slow, employment would shrink, income would fall, and investment would dwindle. The economy could not and would not prosper. This truth is evident throughout most of human history when the world lived in extreme poverty. In the old world of kings ruling, society did not prosper and there was little freedom. Today, autocratic rule, as in Cuba or Venezuela, has left a country that can barely feed itself.

If individuals, workers, and businesses can keep the "fruits of their labor" or get value from their trades, this reward structure provides positive incentive. People will trade, work harder and/or smarter, and be creative as they try to gain the advantage and improve their condition by fulfilling market demand in the most agile and efficient way possible. To do this they must fulfill the demands of the market-place made up of many others who are free to choose to do business with them in voluntary exchanges. The totality of these actions, many pursuing their own interests, spontaneously works to coordinate an economy.

Here's a KISSE: Improvements in society happen when people get to receive the benefits of making those improvements. Consider the washing machine. Utilizing the available resources, individuals like Alva J. Fisher, James King, and Hamilton Smith created a machine that took the laborious task of hand-washing and made it more time efficient. Consumers then bought this machine to benefit their own lives (getting their time back) and the companies that made the machine also benefited (making sales from a service that was in demand and they could supply). This and other innovations free people from mundane labor-intensive chores to do something more productive and rewarding. This adds to prosperity and growth of past and future economies!

Command Economy

The direct opposition to the pure market economy is the command economy. It is commonly referred to as **socialism** or **communism**. Its main characteristic is that government is the primary owner of the means of production. In the 1980s and 1990s, Venezuela was a demand economy, but then socialists took over the country and companies to pay for their welfare programs. As the economy increasingly became more of a socialist economy with socialists running the businesses, the system collapsed.

Karl Marx is the best-known early proponent of socialism (i.e., command economy) as an economic system, as outlined in his classic books *Communist Manifesto* and *Das Kapital*.[3]

Marx's fundamental belief was "from each according to their ability, to each according to their need."[4] In the Marx model of the world, the bourgeoisie (the business owners) and the proletariat (the workers) are at odds and in conflict. According to Marx, business owners exploit their workers by taking from them.

Eventually, the workers rise and take over business, replacing business owners with workers. In this scenario, a small minority with power emerges to serve as a controlling body. This body manages labor, makes production decisions, and runs the economy. However, this was all just theory and didn't work in practice. What evolved was a communist dictatorship, and the working class had less say and autonomy than they did before.

In a command economy, power over resources lies with government officials. They, not the individuals in households nor business owners, must organize and coordinate the production and allocation of all goods and services. The government chooses what to produce, how to produce it, who (both individuals and businesses) gets what, and at what price. Consumers and businesses are largely on the sideline. There is no price signaling to communicate what consumers or businesses want produced and what price they are willing to pay. Everything is left to government planning. Scarce resources are allocated based on what the government officials want produced. They decide how to distribute to the general population. There is no profit motive to guide production decisions and no price signals to communicate what the population values.

All economies are complex. A command economy requires a vast amount of information shared by millions of people to measure the value of available resources. It is unrealistic for the people in government, no matter how well-intentioned, to have enough information or computing power to do everything required to efficiently allocate resources as needed. Rather than relying on the market signals sent by the users of products and services to determine what to bring to consumers or business operators, governments often rely on political signals and other considerations instead. This often leads to cronyism or corruption as the market is not determining the business decisions. This increases the likelihood of significant waste and undertaking counterproductive activities.

With individual business owners, consumers, and workers removed from the process along with prices and profits, there is less reliance on motivation to drive progress, production, and profit, as the positive incentives rewarding wealth creation are essentially eliminated. A command economy relies instead on central planners to focus on production. Since there are less opportunities for labor and entrepreneurship because the fruits of one's efforts are not kept, there is little motivation to work or innovate. Less people will work to advance technology to build a brighter future that spreads wealth across the masses. Thus, fewer overall improvements are made to the country.

This type of command system has never produced desirable results. It has failed to lift millions out of poverty, as contrasted with a market economy. It is, however, a popular idea in some circles, even in the United States, where an increasing number of people have turned to accepting socialism, but many of these people do not fully understand what social-ism really is or the impact it can have on an economy.

Real World Economic Systems

Throughout the world, very rarely is a country's economic system a pure demand or pure command economy. Economies are a blend. Each has a mix of command and demand elements. Some governments will own some factors of production, produce some goods that could have been produced privately, and regulate some markets directly or through price controls.

There are many thoughts and opinions as to the ideal way to structure an economy. Many individuals base their opinions on their **value systems**—the morals, opinions, and beliefs that they use to make decisions—without consideration for alternative values, as to what is the best approach. Rather than a subjective approach to understanding what these different systems mean to individuals living and operating businesses on Main Street, I'll focus on what is different about the overall production levels, employment numbers, income per person, and prices in the two systems.

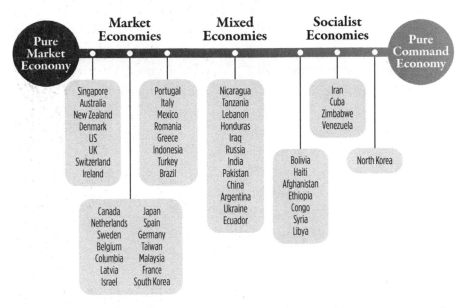

World Economic Systems, 2021

Source: Based on countries' average scores on business, labor, monetary, trade, investment, and financial freedom from the Heritage Foundation's 2021 index of Econorcemic Freedom.

Figure 2.1. This image shows the variety of economics systems around the world and the countries that practice each type. This image shows the variety of economics systems around the world and the countries that practice each type.

The freest economies tend to be market economies. The economic systems of Australia, New Zealand, the United States, the United Kingdom, Ireland, and Canada are the freest, followed by many other European countries as well as East Asian countries' economies. At the other extreme lie the command economies. The tightly controlled economies of Iran, Cuba, Zimbabwe, and Venezuela, which I'll call "socialist economies," are more toward that end, and North Korea is nearly a pure command economy. In the middle are "mixed economies" such as China, Russia, and Vietnam that have significant elements of a market economy but substantial government ownership, direction, and control.

So far, we've been referring to how societies take the productive resources of an economy and combine them into goods and services to define what kind of economic system they are. In doing so, we've compared systems based on whether individuals rely on markets or the government, or a combination of both, to allocate resources to produce goods and services, in what quantities, and how. Countries can also differ in how much government is involved in deciding who gets what and who pays for what they receive. Almost all economies have some form of "social" or welfare programs for its citizens. The nature and scope of these vary widely, even within "market" economies.

Special welfare services may include:
- medical insurance for select groups or for everyone
- healthcare and education
- financing for marginalized communities
- care for elders, children, and the disabled
- food, clothing, and shelter for different groups
- retirement programs such as Social Security

The US is a prime example of mixing market economies with welfare programs. Its list of programs and policies provided by the welfare state is extensive. Programs, such as Social Security and Medicare Part A (hospital insurance coverage), are funded by employers and workers. (However, even today they are not fully funded.) Others are paid for out of general tax revenues on individuals, businesses, estates, and property. The operation, funding, and success of such programs will be covered in later chapters.

Figure 2.2 shows where the United States ranks (thirteenth) in terms of the size of its welfare state against other relatively developed countries, generally other "market" economies. Each bar represents the total percentage of a country's gross domestic product spent on welfare for older citizens, military survivors, those that are mobility challenged, and related benefits—health, family, unemployment, housing, and other social welfare programs.

The Welfare State Across Countries

Gross Public Social Spending as a Percent of GDP, 2019

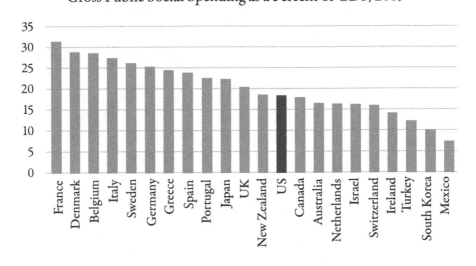

Source: OECD, Social Expenditure(SOCX)Update 2020

Figure 2.2. Countries on the X axis are ordered from the highest to lowest percentage of their country's gross domestic product spent on welfare. Percentages are on the Y axis.

Although the tendency is for free markets to be accompanied by smaller welfare states among these countries, there are notable exceptions: most European countries, as seen above, have large welfare programs but are still very market-oriented economies.

In the welfare state, recipients of welfare- and government-sponsored programs receive benefits if they meet the programs' criteria. These criteria are not driven by profits or competitive prices. They are driven by government policy and the bureaucracy that administers them.

Welfare benefits are funded through the taxes paid either by those receiving benefits or from general revenue of the government. If there is not enough revenue, it is borrowed by the government, thereby committing future generations to pay. In either case, the incentive to be productive and remain competitive is weakened for the taxpayers as well as the welfare recipients, even in a market economy.

The US economy continues to hum along with a 12 percent rate of poverty, making little progress in eradicating it, in spite of the many well-intended programs to reduce poverty.[5] Once the welfare state came into existence and government programs started to bring income into households to feed, clothe, and house individuals and families in the mid-1960s, the progress made in reducing poverty in the US stalled.[6] The incentives that the programs and policies provide motivate people to engage in counterproductive behaviors, instead of rising up and out of poverty. For example, benefits are better for an unmarried couple, so the two-parent household has been significantly reduced. Or benefits are better if you do not earn more money. People often end up dependent on the government for their livelihood because the incentives are misguided.

Each system has its own pros and cons, but in all, the market economy has led to and created the most positives for the most people. A fine balance needs to be struck when considering changes to an economic system, finding what works best for the individuals and the masses, and making adjustments according to what the people and the government can realistically implement and change to further progress.

Next I'll answer the question, "How are resources allocated in an economy?" Is it by markets? By governments? This is the basic economic problem, and the study of how individuals allocate scarce resources to their competing uses is the focus of much of economics.

CHAPTER 3

How Supply and Demand Works

An egg shortage swept the nation in 2022 because of the avian flu. According to data from the US Department of Agriculture, about 60 million birds died as a result of the flu, and the shortage of hens led to cartons of eggs being priced 70 percent higher than normal.[1] This price spike is a result of supply/demand imbalance due to an external event which reduced the supply of eggs—not an inflation-induced event. This is an excellent example (an annoying and expensive one, for those of us that buy eggs) of how supply and demand interact. Resources are always limited in supply. That is the natural condition, but external events can limit it even more, as with the eggs, and the more limited supply will cause prices to rise as explained in this chapter.

Understanding how prices determine the best allocation of scarce resources is a key point in economics, and understanding commonsense economics allows *you* to evaluate what the politicians are talking about and trying to do. Some of their ideas sound good but don't always work to benefit the US economy, you, or your family. Choosing politicians who offer smart, practical economic solutions will improve everyone's standard of living in the US, which improves your life through a firm, common-sense understanding of economics!

Understanding Supply and Demand

"The first lesson of economics is scarcity: there is never enough of anything to satisfy all those who want it. The first lesson of politics is to disregard the first lesson of economics."
—ECONOMIST THOMAS SOWELL[2]

In a market economy such as the United States, the primary mechanism for allocating resources is the free market. A **free market** is where the buyers of goods and services express their needs and desires at various prices—called **demand**—and where sellers express their desires to sell at various prices—called **supply**.

In a world of scarcity, supply and demand interact to determine what price and quantity brings balance between consumers and producers. Price signals convey important information to buyers and sellers, and these signals motivate individuals on both sides of the market to direct scarce resources in ways that are mutually beneficial. And sometimes circumstances can bring about unexpected supply-demand relationships.

When the COVID-19 pandemic spread to the US in 2020, it brought about changes in everyone's day-to-day lives that acted upon the market's supply and demand for certain products and resources. These changes like working from home, masking, and forcing business to shut their doors to the public impacted businesses in ways that, for the most part, could not be predicted. In one case, Andrew—a business owner in Buffalo, New York—worried that the lockdown would mean the end of his music center. Instead, he experienced a unique supply-and-demand phenomenon that brought in more business than he could have anticipated.

Since some people had more time on their hands during lockdown, they were able to both pursue new hobbies and return to old ones, like music. The demand for instruments and their accessories began to skyrocket, reaching the point of extreme supply shortages for Andrew's music center. Instruments need to be carefully crafted and tested before they can ever be sold, and the music center was selling much faster than stock could be replenished. Andrew's team began ordering as much as they could in bulk to meet the needs of new customers. The increase in Andrew's business also caused a demand for him in labor, so he needed more staff to keep up with the orders and test the materials. Andrew was able to expand his staff due to the increase in orders.

Even as the lockdown was lifted, the demand for these products kept up: music concerts were once again taking place, school music programs returned, and people were sustaining their new hobbies. Andrew's business had become a fixed and valued place in his community.

Patterns of demand may be easy to anticipate, or they may react to sudden changes in the broader national landscape. The supply and demand for a product or service can shift in dramatic, unexpected ways at any point, same as with eggs and the avian flu. Businesses like Andrew's must be tuned in to a variety of factors, from their available supply to the market's major price signals.

By looking at the market price, sellers decide how much to sell, and consumers see the available quantities and availability of substitutes, then send out price signals through buying based on their preferences. They allocate their income to achieve the highest possible personal satisfaction.

The role of prices is to simultaneously balance supply and demand in the market. Government interference in the market only distorts these communication channels and price signals. As this book explores later, shortages and surpluses will emerge, along with significant, unintended negative consequences, if there is outside interference in the market.

So now that you understand supply and demand, it's time I throw you a few curves.

Finding Equilibrium on Winding Curves

On the consumer or household's side of the market, there are buyers who are demanding goods and services. A **demand curve** represents the quantities that consumers are willing to purchase at various price points when all other factors affecting demand are held constant. The consumer's relationship with price and quantities are based on common sense. As price increases, quantities demanded decrease and vice versa. This relationship between the price of a good and the quantity demanded is called the **law of demand**.

Law of Demand

When the price of any product increases, then its demand will fall.

Price | Demand

When its price decreases, then its demand will increase in the market.

Price | Demand

Figure 3.1. Arrows illustrate a visual element to the text, showing the relationship between price driving demand.

The desires of sellers are illustrated by the market supply curve for their good or service. A **supply curve** represents the quantities that producers are willing to provide to consumers at various prices. As price increases, profit margins grow and quantities supplied increase. This positive relationship between the price of a good and the quantity supplied is called the **law of supply**.

Law of Supply

According to the law of supply, the higher the price, the larger the quantity produced.

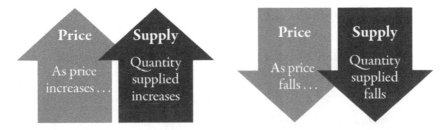

Price — As price increases . . .

Supply — Quantity supplied increases

Price — As price falls . . .

Supply — Quantity supplied falls

Figure 3.2. The first set of arrows demonstrate the idea that increases in prices lead people to produce more. The second set of arrows shows that when a price falls, less is produced.

Where demand and supply meet are the point economists call **market equilibrium**: the quantity demanded equals the quantity supplied at that price point where buyers and sellers are both satisfied given their respective situations, prices, and resources.

Now let's compare oranges to oranges.

At a price of $1 per orange, people will demand three hundred thousand oranges given their incomes and preferences. At a price of $3 per orange, people will demand only one hundred thousand oranges. The higher the price rises for oranges will mean that other things will yield more satisfaction, so fewer oranges and more of other things will be bought.

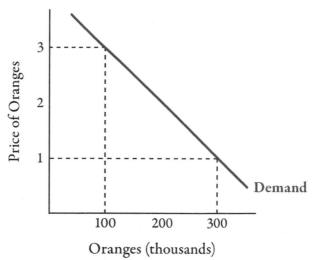

Figure 3.3. The relationship between price and quantity affect how much demand there is for an item.

But say that at a price of $1 per orange, orange growers supply one hundred thousand oranges per day. At a price of $3 per orange, they will supply three hundred thousand oranges. The supply curve will slope upward because more oranges are supplied as the price rises.

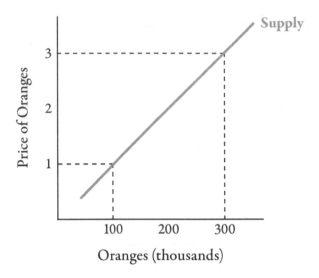

Figure 3.4. Producing less of a good for a lower price leads to a lower supply, while producing more but for more money leads to a higher supply.

Putting our supply and demand curves for oranges together, the equilibrium price is $2, and the equilibrium quantity is two hundred thousand oranges. This equilibrium represents a balance between orange consumers and producers.

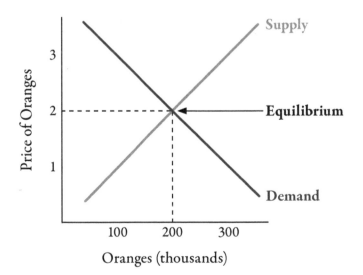

Figure 3.5. The lines from Figure 3.3 and 3.4 are combined to show the equilibrium point between price, demand, and supply.

Changing Equilibrium (The Balance)

Supply and demand are not static. Lots of things can move these curves and create new equilibrium prices. For example, the demand for oranges may go up if new health benefits involving oranges are discovered. This would move the demand curve and create a higher equilibrium price for oranges. On the supply side, if there was a bad winter freeze and the supply of oranges dropped, this would move the supply curve and cause a higher equilibrium price for oranges.

There are lots of factors that can increase or decrease supply and demand—and they would change the market equilibrium price accordingly. The **elasticity of demand** refers to how much a price moves in response to price changes. Demand for a product can be *elastic* (not rigid or constricted and can easily bounce around) or *inelastic* (slow to react).

Gas is probably one of the best inelastic items to talk about. We all need gasoline for our cars. As the supply of gas falls or demand rises, the price will rise. This may cause you to drive less, but you still have to buy gas to drive. So since our need for gas is unavoidable, demand will fall slowly as the price of gas rises, making the demand for this product inelastic. But if we were talking oranges—a commodity you could easily do without or buy something else instead—the rising price would lead to a larger decrease in demand much faster than gas. The demand for this product is elastic.

Interference with Equilibrium

Goods, services, and resources are not always traded as freely as in the examples we've been talking about because, many times, there is interference in the market. Government is the only entity able to interfere in the market. Businesses or consumers acting legally cannot intervene.

Governmental motivations to do something about a particular problem or a crisis often leads to unintended consequences. These unintended consequences stem from attempts to solve one problem by using authority to dictate price. Because such interventions distort price signals, buyers and sellers end up using resources inefficiently, accepting unnecessary risks, and making unsound decisions.

Price Controls

To keep the cost of something "affordable" to people living on lower incomes, a government may come in and enforce **price controls**, which limits the price of a good or service.

In Venezuela, the agricultural sector was taken over by the government and was run very poorly. Their efforts failed and caused shortages of flour and toilet paper, which drove up the price of each significantly. The government solution was to put price controls on these and other items, thereby limiting—by law—what producers could charge. When the price was below the equilibrium, producers did not offer enough to satisfy what consumers want, so the result was a shortage of bread and toilet paper in Venezuela. If the price had gone below the cost of production, none would have been offered. The result is the opposite of what was intended.[3]

Closer to home, a particularly devastating government intervention is rent control. This policy is intended to make housing more affordable for low-income families by setting maximum rent levels. But in response to rent controls, landlords reduce the amount of rental housing available to this group. This movement creates a shortage of "affordable" housing. This is the opposite of what is intended. Rent controls also have additional harmful effects in the long run because the landlords cannot build up reserves to improve their properties, which means rent-controlled properties are more likely to deteriorate over time.[4]

Underground Black Markets

When government interference creates shortages, as in the Venezuela example above, "illegal" markets outside of the government's sight often arises. The same can happen in our own country. Massachusetts banned the sale of menthol cigarettes in June of 2020, and in April 2021, the federal Food and Drug Administration (FDA) announced its plan to impose a national ban on menthol cigarettes. Some critics predict a prohibition, if such a measure is approved, will create illicit manufacturing that will lead to menthol cigarettes being sold illegally in **underground markets** or **black markets**. This is the place where, or system by which, the producers sell their product to meet the demand that is not met in the restricted, legal markets. Sellers in underground markets can get higher prices to cover costs and make a profit. These black markets balance supply and demand, but at a higher price to consumers.

This underground alternative will not satisfy the government's objective of getting goods to low-income people, but it helps alleviate the government-created shortages. Without an underground market, there would be less available for everyone, the exact opposite of the intentions of government. Government interference does not yield the results desired, no matter how well-intended the policies are. Even with an underground market, the shortages still exist and not everyone will have the amount they want.

Price Floors

On the other side of the equation, governments often set **price floors** for some commodities, such as milk and other agricultural goods, to boost incomes for farmers. A price floor is a price set above the free-market price. Prices above the equilibrium price will lead producers to make more than consumers want to buy. So there is an unwanted supply (surplus) in the market at an artificially higher price.

You might have heard of "government cheese," but you might not know that the story of government cheese begins with the federal government's policies to maintain the price of milk above the free-market price. The government's solution to this problem was to buy up the surplus milk in the form of cheese, butter, and powdered milk because these products can be stored more easily than milk. At one point, government cheese was stored in hundreds of warehouses across the country, amounting to about two pounds of cheese for every person in the country. The government even began distributing the cheese in large blocks to welfare and food stamp recipients to reduce its cheese mountain.

Although the objective of boosting farmers' incomes was met, the price floor made milk and other dairy products more expensive for consumers, led to reduced consumption of milk products, and created a surplus of milk that had to be bought with our tax money and warehoused for years before rotting or being given away. In short, the government and its policy involved negative consequences for everyone, except for those farmers benefiting from the price supports.

Government Regulations

Government licensing and compliance regulations are a cost of doing business. In a normal environment, this is business as usual and is expected to a reasonable extent. But sometimes these are so burdensome and costly, it significantly impacts the marketplace.

For example, it takes years and significant regulatory costs to permit a new mine or a nuclear power plant. In California, marijuana was legalized, but the permitting and regulations are so burdensome and costly, there has been a much lower number of producers than expected, driving up the price. This has in turn led to some underground markets for the sale of marijuana where the "illegal" sellers are not burdened with the high cost of government regulations and can be sold at lower prices.

Separating intentions from consequences is important. Economists must analyze the policies and incentives created by government officials to foresee the likely results—which often are the opposite of the stated intentions. Policy that sounds good politically is often harmful for the economy and its citizens after the intended and unintended consequences are considered. Factoring in the existing supply and demand climate for each change will help our government make more informed decisions on what steps they do take to regulate the economy in a way that still allows the economy to run itself efficiently and supply the people with what they demand.

Which do you want more?

CHAPTER 4

Key Ideas in Modern Economics

Now knowing the systems and curves that influence our decision-making on the day-to-day and how those are impacting us in our choices, it's plain to see that we, as consumers, interact with economics every day—each time we make a decision. How you choose what you choose has an economic impact on what you do, how your life turns out, and how your future is set up. This is the basic of opportunity cost, and it's one of the main ideas in today's economics that I'll go over in this chapter along with defining the differences between absolute advantage and comparative advantage. I'll talk about economics of scale, diminishing returns, and marginal utility.

Opportunity Costs

If you have an opportunity to do something or buy something, and you do it, you have given up the opportunity to do/buy something else. The **opportunity cost** is the cost of what you did not do or buy. This is what a person sacrifices when they choose one option over another, the value of the next best choice. You have limited time in your day and can do only one thing at a time (multitasking is manageable in very specific circumstances). There are many choices on how to spend your time. If you are thinking of either going to the movies or going ice skating or taking a nap, and you choose the movie, the cost of going to the movie is not going ice skating or catching up on probably much-needed sleep. Or suppose you have a choice to work or play tennis. If you don't go to work and choose instead to play tennis, then you won't get the money you would've earned, which is considered a lost opportunity cost.

For example, we have finite resources in money, goods, and time. If we have $2 and we want a loaf of bread, and we choose to buy it, that means: First, you valued the bread more than you valued the $2 in a free exchange. Second, the opportunity cost of the bread was the cost of, say, the candy that you did not buy. The cost of the bread was the opportunity cost to buy candy instead since you only had $2 and chose the bread.

Some choices hold much greater cost considerations. Many adults, for instance, must decide at some point in their lives if they want to enter higher education or the workforce—and such a decision demands serious risk- and opportunity-cost considerations.

In an interview featured in national economic news coverage, Shannon of Des Moines, Iowa, expressed how she knew when she was in middle school that she wanted to dedicate her life to the field of medicine. After struggling in higher-level science classes, however, she felt pressured to give up that future and focus her life on other pursuits. She went on to marry her husband at a young age, and when the couple added two children to their family, she found herself in a situation where she needed a career that would allow her to help provide for them financially. While she could have found a job that did not require further education, she took the opportunity to begin nursing school instead.

Shannon was scared. Nursing school was a risk. If it didn't work out, she would lose the time and resources that nursing school demanded and would find herself back at square one. As a result of that risk though, Shannon found success in both her academic and career pursuits. She graduated, got a job, and could provide for her family to better their future. Shannon was able to send her daughter to college without worrying about student loan debt.

The cost of going to nursing school and becoming certified was, primarily, the loss of immediate employment for Shannon—but in the long run, the cost of the opportunity she may have lost was greatly outweighed by the benefits of her decision.

There's a lot of ways we can see this at play in our lives, like competing job offers, investing in the stock market or relying on the interest from a savings account, choosing to spend money on travel or career development courses—even buying that $1 snack from a fast-food place instead of saving it for another day. Opportunity is everywhere. We just have to figure out how much it costs and if we're willing to spend.

Absolute and Comparative Advantage

For a sound understanding of economics, the next two ideas are critical. The overall concept of "advantage" is simple—when something is better or more efficient than another thing. It's great. Everyone loves to have advantage.

But comparative and absolute advantage are a bit different. **Comparative advantage** factors in opportunity costs and advises how trading partners can help each other by specializing the production of goods in which they are low-cost producers and trading with others for the products they do not produce. **Absolute advantage** does not factor in opportunity cost. It is simply a reflection of who is the absolute lowest or best producer of a product.

Think about it this way. Even though a person, business, or country is more efficient in all things, the total output is greater if they spend time and resources on what they do the most efficiently (the comparative advantage) and the less efficient producers will do other items, even though they are less efficient. By doing this, the total economic output is maximized for the benefit of all.

For example, if John can make sixteen shirts per hour and Joe can only make eight, John has an absolute advantage in shirtmaking. That's easy. If John can make eight shoes per hour and Joe can only make six, John has an absolute advantage in shoemaking. That's easy too. But . . . John and Joe have a limited amount of time and resources and can only work for an hour. If they each split their time/resources and make both, John will make eight shirts and four shoes and Joe will make four shirts and three shoes. The total output is twelve shirts and seven shoes (nineteen units).

If John spends all his time on shirts and Joe spends all his time on shoes, there will be sixteen shirts and six shoes (or total output of twenty-two units). The total output is greater. Why? Because John has a comparative advantage by the greater efficiency he has in making shirts versus the lesser advantage he has in making shoes. The net result by allocating resources to the most efficient producer of an item results in greater overall production.

Economies of Scale/Diminishing Returns/Marginal Utility

As a general concept, as an enterprise grows, the cost of production declines. This is called the **economies of scale**, and it happens when it costs a company less to make a single product as output increases.

Why? Because as they grow there can be more efficiency in production, and the cost per unit will decline as efficiency increases. Part of this is due to fixed costs that can be spread out over more items, making the fixed cost per unit go down. But there are also efficiencies that can be obtained in the variable costs as we grow and utilize more efficient equipment, manpower can be specialized and more efficient, or we can buy raw materials in volume at lower costs.

But this is not unlimited. At some point, the **marginal utility**—the output "at the margin" or how much output you can get from the next unit of production—of the next unit can decrease. If the **marginal utility** starts to go down, you have **diminishing returns**, which means there is less profit from the next unit of production than you have when you are at the optimal production level.

If the focus is on hitting the lowest cost per unit, there will be a point in which adding production costs more than the added output. At that point, you have crossed the line where total costs start to increase. At this point, you have passed peak efficiency.

Balancing out all these factors—the opportunities, advantages, scales, utilities, and returns—are essential to running a business, and economy, in a way that sets it up for long-term success.

"I feel like we've bought one of those every year since 1976."

CHAPTER 5

All About Profit, Competition, and Creative Destruction

In Chapter 3, we went over how market prices balance the benefits from the things people buy against the costs of producing them. On the supply side, sellers are motivated by the pursuit of profit and compete for your business. In working for their self-interest, they are working for yours, too, and are solving the problem of scarcity as scarce resources are allocated through market forces. This might be the most important, yet underappreciated, feature of a market economy, so it's worth diving into it a bit more.

Profits

In a free-market economy, profits are realized by satisfying consumers at acceptable prices. These are what we will call **principled profit**, which is an essential motivator in a market-based economy. When a producer collects more revenue than it pays in costs, they see a profit. Profit is the incentive, and incentives are key to motivate people's actions.

Businesses work to bring in profits for owners and investors. Entrepreneurs take on the risk of starting and running a business and its profits that incentivize them to satisfy consumers at agreeable prices. But there is no guarantee of success. Many businesses fail. So anticipating how to satisfy consumers at acceptable prices which yield a profit is the key to success.

An interview with Anna of Nashua, New Hampshire, revealed the function of profit as a key benefit for both her business and the community it serves. Anna helps run an early-childhood education center founded by her mother, but the start of the COVID-19 pandemic indicated serious trouble for the family business. At the time, she saw no other course of action but to close the center's doors and work on developing new health and safety training procedures, and though the business proved to be adaptable in this regard, its eventual reopening was disrupted by high staff-turnover rates. The work had become more difficult, and the environment had changed. Former employees before the pandemic were not sticking around.

Anna had to find another solution to ensure the health of her business. She researched the minimum living pay of her town and made the decision to match that threshold in the wages the center offered; its child-care-paying employees could then work full time at her company without needing to work other jobs to sustain themselves.

The center raised its tuition in reflection of these higher labor costs, ensuring their finances could continue to sustain a living wage for its staff. While early-childhood education has become a steep expense for many US families, Anna remains committed to finding ways to make their services more accessible to lower-income families, all while balancing the delicate relationship between their tuition and their wages.

In this case, the business's profit was able to feed back into its operations and better enrich the experience of its employees and, in turn, its clients. Its incentive was more than monetary: the generation of profit ensured that the center could adapt to a major environmental change and remain in operation, providing a key service to the community it belongs to. In responding to the market and its needs, the business can thrive.

But there is no guarantee that business will experience success. Many, many businesses fail. So anticipating how to satisfy consumers at acceptable prices in a dynamic marketplace is key.

So how does all this pursuit of profit benefit you and society as a whole? If a seller is trying to maximize profit, he's also trying to provide as much benefit to consumers relative to the cost of making the good.

Competition

To obtain the best results for consumers, the profit motive is guided by the forces of market **competition**. We can think of competition as the guardrails that keep profit-seeking sellers focused on offering the most value to buyers at the lowest possible costs.

A typical transaction in the marketplace involves mutually advantageous trade. Two or more parties voluntarily exchange goods, services, or money to gain value relative to what they give up. For example, if you buy a $2 loaf of bread from a baker, it must mean that you place a value of at least $2 on the bread. Correspondingly, the baker sells the bread for more than what it cost him to make and pockets a profit. Both buyer and seller are happy.

Although the baker in the example is happy, he cannot be complacent because things can quickly change for the worse. The resources he uses to make bread are in limited supply and producers of other goods might outbid him to get those resources. The demand for bread can decrease at any time and the new market price might not be high enough for him to make a profit.

But this can also go the other way. Breadmaking could become even more profitable, and new producers might enter the market, increasing the supply of bread and lowering the equilibrium price. If the new producers are more efficient than some of the existing producers, the least efficient will exit the bread business. Our baker needs to be sure that he is not one of them.

Like every producer, our baker is in competition with everyone else in the economy, and he uses prices to help decide what to do. Since the marketplace is where prices are set, competition directs producers to the most efficient allocation of resources. Suppliers stop using and providing scarce resources in markets in which there is no longer demand. Resources will be directed elsewhere in the pursuit of profits and keeping doors opened and employees paid.

· ·

"It is not from the benevolence of the butcher,
the brewer, or the baker that we expect our dinner,
but from their regard to their own interest."
—ADAM SMITH[1]

· ·

We are discussing this as if competition is perfect, but so often it isn't. Buyers and sellers do not know all the facts. Property rights are not always clearly defined. Circumstances can change. Markets fail. Government promises and then doesn't deliver.

Take, for example, the COVID-19 pandemic, which led governments nationwide to order closures so that Americans could avoid getting sick and spreading the infection. Some retail stores—Bed Bath & Beyond, Walmart, Gap, Party City, Macy's, Big Lots, JCPenney, etc.—still haven't fully recovered from the 2020–2022 disruption and were forced to close some of their retail stores. And although most have escaped bankruptcy for now, Bed Bath & Beyond is reportedly cutting its number of store-fronts from 1,500 to 480 and is now bankrupt.[2]

These and other factors affect demand, supply, pricing, and equilibrium between buyers and sellers. But the key point is that when competition is at its best, free markets extract the most benefits for consumers from an efficient allocation of scarce resources. And all this happens because the sellers are trying to get as much profit as possible.

Creative Destruction

Competition is not just about providing given goods at the lowest cost, but also about *which* goods will be provided. Firms will compete with one another by charging lower prices, offering more desirable varieties, and creating new goods with new ways to deliver them.

Creative destruction is what keeps the economy growing and advancing: as businesses innovate in a competitive market, new features or products are developed to satisfy consumers, and old features and goods are discarded.[3]

Cell phones are a great example of creative destruction. Like television sets, they were unimaginable, except for in science fiction fifty years ago. The first ones were bulky and limited in features. As a new product, it didn't replace any existing products. But then new features were added, and old products became obsolete. When the Blackberry became a very popular smartphone, it made the clunkier phone models obsolete. The same is true for TV consoles. Flat-screen televisions have replaced cathode-ray tube TV.

After the Blackberry phone, the Apple iPhone improved smartphones even more. Slowly, most Blackberry phones became largely obsolete. Apple was so successful that competition with it arose to improve features and lower costs. The iPhone continued to improve and now there are many successful competitors in the market. The old products were driven from the market as better, more innovative products were developed. That is, old products underwent creative destruction because of the new and better products.

Just as everyone has a phone in their pocket instead of a clunky landline, computers have displaced the typewriter, cars have replaced the horse and buggy, petroleum has replaced whale oil, and so on.

There have been countless once-thriving firms, industries, and jobs that have been "destroyed" every time a new product replaced an old one. Remember Blockbuster Video stores? They were replaced by Netflix in 2014.

—$$$—

Profits and competition are a crucial incentive in a free-enterprise/market economy. Those are the key elements that foster growth, innovation, and improvements in our standard of living. They are the "unintended consequences" of the "invisible hand" at work, promoting the common good.

The process of innovation and creativity will cause capital to flow from one industry to another, with an attendant dislocation of workers and capital. This is a normal process in a growing economy and results in improving standards of living for all.

. . . .

"Consumption is the sole end and purpose of all production."
—ADAM SMITH[4]

. . . .

"Oh no, it's not stealing. It's eminent domain."

CHAPTER 6

Key Stuff:
Private Property and the Rule of Law

The debate about whether private property is better than common property for society and the common person can be traced back to Plato and Aristotle.[1] Plato believed that property held in common was best for everyone, but Aristotle (his student) argued the opposite and claimed that privately owned property being traded voluntarily in the marketplace was the ideal. That argument continues to this day. To understand this debate fully, it's important to know what is meant by the term "property."

Private and Common Property

We hear about private property all the time, but what is it really? And what's its alternative? That would be **common property**, which is when property is not owned by anyone but the "group," whereas **private property** means that someone owns the property and has rights in it. With private property, others do not have right to buy, use, sell, or derive income from that property other than the private individual who owns it. Not only do the owners have rights to their private property, but they can also transfer rights of ownership to others in exchange for something they value more, like payment, other types of property, or services.

The three key elements to private property ownership include
1. exclusive use of the property or labor;
2. legal possession and protection from outsiders; and
3. freedom to exchange property (or labor) with others.

Property includes those tangibles that you own—your house, land, phone, vehicle, and other tangibles.

It also includes your labor for which you can exchange for wages and salaries, such as intellectual property, or knowledge derived from your work. Property can be protected by agreements, contracts, or patents.

The important thing about property and prosperity is people can trade in mutually advantageous ways—in the spirit of cooperation and through harmonious action and interaction. Trading, saving, investing, and innovating stem from powerful incentives which allow persons, communities, and nations to flourish. Take away those incentives and economies struggle, and people hide what they and others value and want. This requires **rule of law** (as mentioned in Chapter 2), which protects your rights from excessive or arbitrary use of power by putting in place an established set of rules and is a basic requirement for private property.

Rule of Law

The governing body in a society has a basic core function: to establish a set of rules and laws for the society. Under the rule of law, boundaries are enforced equally and do not vary arbitrarily from person to person nor are they based on who knows who nor when not to enforce rules. All people and institutions are subject to and accountable to laws that are fairly applied and enforced. There is, ideally, no one who is "above" the law. These rules are the Golden Rule codified: "Do unto others as you would have them do unto you." Others might characterize this as the "natural right" to property you properly own. I cannot take what is yours if you cannot take what is mine.

Let's look at this in a bit more detail.

Imagine a place where rulers have the power to take your property for reasons undisclosed. Knowing that whatever you owned or had that others valued could be taken from you, wouldn't you be discouraged from investing, saving in banks, and innovating in that area since your property is subject to the whims of the rulers? Would you want to stay, invest, and trade in this area? My guess is probably not. But what if you had another location to move to, one that had outlined clear and protected rights to property and had the rule of law? Would you not care for and maintain your property, whether for your own benefit or for a burgeoning business? It's not guards but the rule of law that protects your property and your neighbor's property in an evenhanded fashion. This is the incentive for you to use your resources properly: You are protected, and *you* benefit. Where property is commonly owned, this incentive is destroyed.

Centrally planned economies with arbitrary rules show why economies and standards of living didn't develop until secure property rights across populations were established. Property rights do not exist in anarchy or under rule by force. They only exist when there is rule of law. Rule of law also applies to all physical and intellectual property and "rights." Contracts give rise to "rights" between the parties and are based on conditions that all agree on. These rights must be, and are, protected as well.

To enforce these rules, a system must exist to bring rule breakers and exploiters to account. In a modern society, that requires a police force and judicial system. The police force can establish, if there is solid evidence, that a rule has been breached, and the judicial system interprets the laws, defends them, and rules on how to settle a dispute or resolve a conflict. To pay for this protection, government, and enforcement of the rule of law, the system has the right to tax and receive revenue from its citizens. To be effective, the rules and enforcement must be reliable. When they are, the environment is right for people to flourish since they are protected from arbitrary plunder by thugs, mobs, corrupt businesses, authoritarian government agencies, or kings and queens.

When a society has individual rights and property secure and protected, all people are free to engage in economic activity. Individuals, business owners, and companies can invest knowing their property is secure. This is a key element. In a developing community or society, economic activity can flourish and grow when businesses can invest, improve products, and lower the costs of delivering goods or services since they trust that they, their property, and profits are safe and protected. These benefits spill over to prosperity for the entire population.

While limited government helps an economy function, too much taxation, government borrowing, and regulation create disincentives to trade, invest, save, and innovate. When laws are punitive and overly disincentivize commerce, they largely work against the growth and prosperity of society by marginalizing the working class and especially those living in marginalized communities.

—$$$—

Property rights and the rule of law are essential ingredients for a well-functioning economy. This allows people the freedom to invest with confidence that prosperity for one will multiply and benefit the many.

CHAPTER 7

The Excitement of Governing and Government Policy

In all societies there is either some form of governing body or there is anarchy. The "society" can be a democratically elected republic as in the US or an autocratically ruled country such as China or a remote village in Africa with its chosen tribal leaders. Even when there is no official governing body, eventually someone seizes control and "governs" in some form, be it civilly (with consent of the governed) or by brute force. How a government acts impacts us all.

In today's world, a governing body of some sort exists pretty much everywhere. While there may be dissidents or wars to change who governs, there is still someone or some group that makes policy decisions for the society at any given moment in time.

What is Government?

In its most elemental form, a **government** is an organization of people that exists to oversee and lead others in a direction set by those who govern. It can be for the common good and functions to protect the rights among those in the country, state, or community being governed (with civil democracies, change occurs by the vote of the public) or it can also be set up for the benefit of those with power and control, in an autocratic state ruled by force. In autocracies, change occurs by conflict and overthrow of the autocracy.

In a democratic republic, citizens vote for which representatives get to govern. It is, therefore, the citizens who elect those who most closely represent what the public majority wants. The elected officials are responsible to the voters to represent the views of those who placed them in office. The Preamble to the US Constitution sets forth the groundwork for these functions of our government:

· ·

"We the people of the United States, in Order to form a more perfect Union, establish Justice, ensure domestic Tranquility, provide for the common defense, promote the general Welfare, and secure the Blessings of Liberty to ourselves and our Posterity, do ordain and establish this Constitution for the United States of America." —THE PREAMBLE TO THE US CONSTITUTION[1]

· ·

So then what are the typical functions of government? Government influences how a country or group fares economically and how well the people live. So it's important to know which types and approaches of government are best for guiding how well a society lives and functions today and in the future.

The bottom line is that there is no pure form of government. The same holds true in market or command economies. There are many gradations between the two extremes and even under an autocracy, the rulers can choose to employ techniques of a market economy or essentially be a command economy (China and Vietnam are examples of current world autocracies with some significant elements of a market economy).

Government and the Economy

Typically, there are two types: large government and limited government. In a **large government**, there are more public workers, more government intervention in the public and private sector, and more establishments of catch-all entities that would absorb what could come out of a competing private entity. This typically means a bigger social safety net, higher taxes, and more interventions in private businesses. **Limited government** sees less regulation and involvement from a state, which means there are fewer public programs (i.e., less public workers), so there are less guaranteed, sustained jobs. There are always dislocations, and government workers eventually find jobs in the productive sector, which grows when the government decreases in size. Smaller government also means less capital taken from private sources, leaving more room for more private investment in a growing economy.

What do economists mean when they say "limited government"? Do they want no government? Of course not. Economists recognize the importance of government; in fact, economic freedom rises with the quality of the legal system, market freedom, and constrained taxation and government spending. Adam Smith in his classic work on economics *An Inquiry into the Nature and Causes of the Wealth of Nations* assigns three main functions to government:[2]

1. National defense;
2. administration of justice; and
3. provision of certain public goods.

Limited (small) government, as laid out by Smith, helps a civil society grow and prosper by

1. defending its people from aggression;
2. creating and enforcing laws for the protection of all people, property, and natural rights;
3. providing an unbiased judiciary system to rule on the laws;
4. supplying those few services difficult for markets to produce for the common good;
5. managing those parts of economy subject to market failures;
6. collecting taxes to pay for the cost of government and the services it provides; and
7. offering a safety net for individuals in need.

Let's look at these ideas from Smith in action. A useful measure of government intervention is provided by the Fraser Institute (Figure 7.1), which considers the list of seven roles for government to create an index of economic freedom. It shows how economic well-being, as measured by average income within a country, relates to the amount of government a country has.

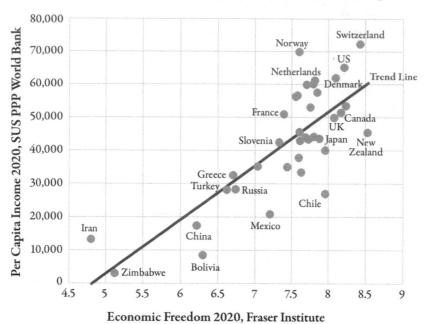

Figure 7.1. The dots surrounding the upward trending line represent countries' economic freedom versus individual wages. Switzerland is at the highest, with Iran at the lowest. Most countries' people earn around 40k to 60k in income and have between a 7 to 8.5 on the economic freedom scale.

We can follow that red trendline and see that the more economic freedom a country has, the more a person will make in a year (i.e., the higher economic well-being), which leads to a stronger economy. It is important, therefore, to be vigilant in protecting economic freedom while providing necessary government services. Some examples that we can see a history of this relationship between government and economic freedom are China and Vietnam. They are current world autocracies with some significant elements of a market economy, but in the past, these economies were primarily command economies, which trapped the people living in the general population in extreme poverty. The government blocked both access to global markets and growth in capital markets, extinguished entrepreneurship, and more.

Eventually, enlightened autocrats entered government and liberalized the economies with some market economic principles. After liberalization and open trade with other countries, different pockets of people began to prosper with increasing incomes. In other command countries, such as North Korea or Cuba, this transformation to include liberalized market-economic principles has been denied to the people. Poor living conditions, bad health, substandard education, denied access to technology and modern communication, and low levels of income continue to plague country residents. So the general population continues to suffer, and they continue to lag behind others. The policy choices we face in the United States are nowhere as dramatic as those faced by the citizens living in China and Vietnam or North Korea and Cuba. But it is important to understand the proper role of government and how that role affects well-being even in relatively prosperous market economies like the United States.

Economic well-being is affected by more than government policy and markets—there are also other factors. Differences in history, social considerations, geography, natural resources, and any number of other things also can explain these variances. Oil-rich Norway can have a higher average income than the US despite having less economic freedom, while remote New Zealand with its vibrant heritage can have more economic freedom but still not be able to achieve the US's average income.

Governments, politicians, and policies can and do fail just like markets. Economics and critical thinking shed light on why this reality matters and reveals how unconstrained political processes, not markets, are responsible and can be held accountable for income inequalities, wage discrimination, keeping people in poverty, tax distortions, political favoritism, monopolies, high prices, and more.

Frédéric Bastiat, a noted nineteenth-century classical liberal econo-mist, describes the one key difference between a good and bad economist.

. . . .

"Between a good and a bad economist this constitutes
the whole difference—the one takes account of the visible effect;
the other takes account both of the effects which are seen and
also of those which it is necessary to foresee."
— **Frédéric Bastiat**[3]

. . . .

This same statement applies to politicians. What I'm asking of, and writing for, is for everyone (the "voting public") to understand the truth versus fairy dust and vote intelligently for politicians who understand and explain the "seen and the unseen" implications of policies they promote. Economic policies frequently lead to sometimes disastrous unforeseen events, resulting in people facing the unintended consequences of the mishaps or undelivered promises of government. This book aims to reveal both the intended and unintended consequences of the policy promise of elected officials and policy makers. The implications for today and the future are deserving of your attention. It is the results that matter, not the intentions, both in the long run as well as today.

—$$$—

In upcoming chapters, we will explore how to use economic principles in a market economy with different levels of government involvement in various aspects of citizens' lives. This exploration will highlight how markets and government work in tandem to improve or take away from people's well-being. A theme that will appear regularly is how a few simple economic principles can unlock the mysteries of the markets and government policies. Voters, or anyone following fiscal, monetary, or trade policy, will understand these hot topics by simply knowing both the seen and the unseen effects of good versus bad economic policy.

CHAPTER 8

What the Heck Is Macroeconomics?

We previously learned about microeconomics: the study of how individuals and business functions. This chapter is all about **macroeconomics**, which is the study of how the overall economy operates. Macroeconomics is divided into two general categories: (1) **monetary policy**, which is the managing of money supply and interest rates, and (2) **fiscal policy**, the managing of income and expenses of government.

In this chapter we will focus on measuring the economy, some of the key terms you hear every day and what they mean, how we compare to other countries, and how government policies affect the overall economy. In later chapters we will dive deeper into monetary/fiscal policy and international trade.

National Income and Inflation

The broadest measure of the size of a nation's economy is **gross domestic product** (GDP), which is the total value of goods and services produced during a year. Since the goods and services produced are purchased by people and businesses, GDP is also the total income received by people in the country. The amount of goods and services produced/sold per person (per capita) in real terms is a good measure of the standard of living for the residents of that country. When we say *real terms*, it means the actual (real) amount of goods and services that can be consumed, not just in monetary terms.

Here's a KISSE: If you translate dollars into UK pounds, it might be $2.00 is the same as 1.47 pounds. But if a loaf of bread costs $2.00 here and there it costs 2 pounds, their money buys less as 2 pounds is the same as $2.71. So in "real" terms, bread is more expensive there.

Inflation is also a factor when comparing national income year to year. To compare data, typically there will be a base year used and all monetary data is adjusted to be consistent with the base year, which eliminates the distortion of inflation.

Figures 8.1 and 8.2 below put the US economy into perspective. The first chart shows that the US economy is easily the largest in the world, accounting for about 24 percent of the entire world's economy. China and the European Union are the next two largest economies, each being about three-quarters of the size of the US economy.

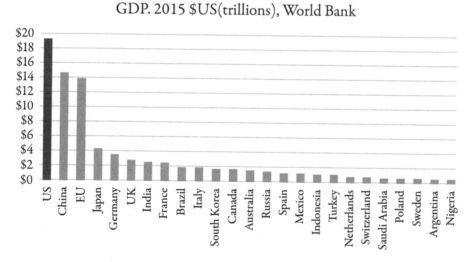

Twenty-Five Largest Economies in 2020
GDP. 2015 $US(trillions), World Bank

Figure 8.1. The US has the largest economy, followed by China, then the EU. A sharp drop between the EU's GDP and Japan's GDP (ranked third and fourth, respectively) shows that the first three economies account for a majority of the world's GDP.

The US economy is large, but that does not tell the whole story. To gauge the standard of living in a country, we use **consumption per person**, in which the total economic output is divided by the population to determine the output per person (per capita). The United States provides a very high average income for its residents.

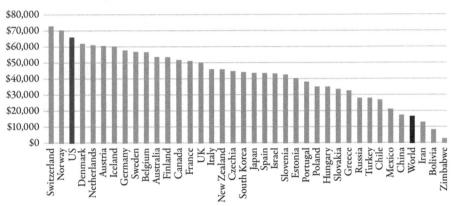

Per Capita Income 2020, SUS PPP, World Bank

Figure 8.2. Population size heavily impacts a citizen's income in each country. Compared to Figure 8.1., the US is third for per capita income, while China comes thirty-fourth out of thirty-eight places. Switzerland is now ranked number one, compared to it's twentieth-ranked spot of twenty-five in Figure 8.1.

As Figure 8.2 shows, per capita GDP in the US is about four times that of the world. China's economy, as seen in Figure 8.1, while large, provides an average income that is just slightly above the world average. This means that the standard of living in the US is about four times higher than that in China or the average of the world.

. . . .

"Inflation is always and everywhere a monetary phenomenon.
—MILTON FRIEDMAN[1]

. . . .

Inflation occurs when there are ongoing price increases for goods and services. Even though prices are in constant flux, that doesn't necessarily mean that inflation is happening. Price changes must occur broadly across goods and services for the situation to be called inflation, which is also often described as "too much money chasing too few goods."

To monitor and detect inflation, policymakers use several measures of the price level. The best known measure is the **consumer price index** (CPI). Roughly speaking, the CPI is the average price of a bundle of goods that the typical household might purchase. The inflation rate is the percentage change in the CPI over the previous year.

When trying to detect true inflation, analysts might look at core CPI, which excludes changes in food and energy prices. Prices of those goods, particularly energy, are relatively volatile and might cloud the picture of the general change in prices.

The Federal Reserve sets targets for inflation, interest rates, and monetary growth. Inflation affects everyone in the economy and can be especially hard on those whose incomes are not keeping up with rising prices, such as those on fixed incomes. If inflation rates are higher than growth rates of income, the "real" standard of living has decreased. For people on fixed incomes, their money buys less, resulting in a lower standard of living.

It is monetary policy—rapid growth in the money supply—that causes inflation. For example, if you double the amount of money in the economy and the amount of goods does not change, then the prices of all goods will approximately double to absorb all the extra dollars. Why? With more money, people will want to buy more (demand) at the lower price. As discussed in Chapter 3, at lower prices there would be a shortage of goods. Accordingly, the prices will be bid up until equilibrium is reached at approximately double the price. This does not mean prices are static when there is no or low inflation. Changing supply and demand for specific items will cause price changes constantly—going up and down.

Economic Growth

Economic growth is generally a good thing: The faster GDP rises in real terms, the larger the economy gets and the standard of living for the average person increases. Thus, **economic growth** is measured in terms of real GDP, which is simply GDP that eliminates the impact of inflation.

Figure 8.3 below shows how real GDP has tended to rise over time and is about six times what it was in 1960. The economy experiences a business cycle that includes episodes during which real GDP falls before recovering and returning to its upward trend. These periods of negative growth are called **recessions**. In the chart, the eight recessions that the US economy experienced between 1961 and 2021 are shaded gray.

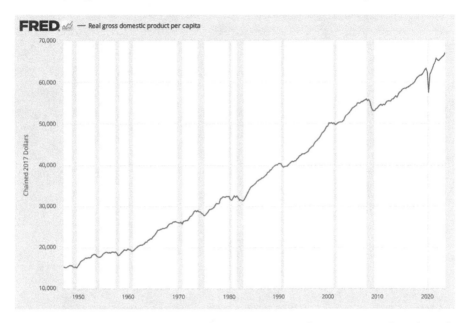

**Sources: Data from U.S. Bureau of Economic Analysis (2023);
Image from FRED, Federal Reserve Bank of St. Louis (2023).**

Figure 8.3. The GDP per capita is charted from the mid-twentieth century to the present with the chained value of the 2017 US dollar. The periods of negative growth—recessions—are shaded gray, accompanied by drops in the GDP's upward trend.

It's convenient to think of economic growth in terms of the long and short run. In the long run, economic growth is determined by productivity, investment in resources of production, proper institutions, and sound economic policies. In the short run, recessions might occur as the result of unanticipated disruptions like oil shocks, financial crises, pandemics, or actions of the government. Macroeconomic policies can, therefore, differ a great deal depending on where the economy is in its business/economic cycle.

Unemployment and Jobs

Other common indicators of how the macroeconomy is doing are the unemployment rate and job growth. They provide good measures of how the economy is performing and are used as measures of how the economy is affecting people directly. Both measures are based on surveys: the unemployment rate is from a survey of households and job growth is from a survey of employers.

Every month, the Bureau of Labor Statistics (BLS) surveys about sixty thousand households across the US. The questions include whether people in the household are employed, unemployed (not employed but looking for work), or consider themselves out of the labor force (neither employed nor looking to be employed). The labor force includes those who are employed or unemployed, and the unemployment rate is the share of the labor force that is unemployed.

As you can see in Figure 8.4, the unemployment rate rises rapidly during a recession and falls (often slowly) as the economy recovers.

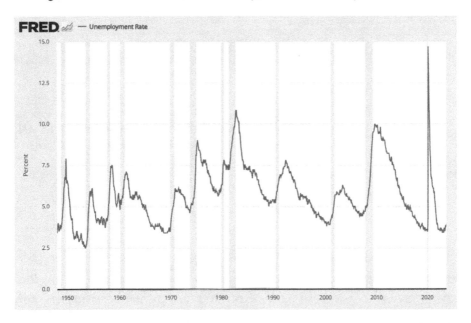

Sources: Data from U.S. Bureau of Labor Statistics (2023);
Image from FRED, Federal Reserve Bank of St. Louis (2023).

Figure 8.4. The chart illustrates the relationship between periods of recession and spikes in the rate of unemployment.

This information serves as a vital economic indicator, but it is important to note that the meaning employment surveys offer is always dependent on a broader societal context. Such as in the case of Jordan, a marketing professional of Silver Spring, Maryland, and his mom. Jordan's mother recently re-entered employment, but not because she was eager for work. Approaching seventy years old and already in retirement, she began to struggle to cover bills and regular expenses and needed a way to secure income to stay afloat. Jordan has a job he loves that pays well, but he can only contribute so much to his mother's situation while he still has his own expenses, like daily living and student loan debt, to pay. He may help with cell phone and cable bills, but major expenses are not something he can plan for; his mother's need for a job felt unavoidable. From Jordan's perspective, job reports do little to indicate the sacrifices individuals may be making by having to seek employment. His situation demonstrates that from some's perspective, more people entering the work force is not always a clear indicator of a healthy economy.

Macroeconomics considers the unemployment rate to understand how many people who are looking for work can find it, but it is not a direct measure of individual hardship. Rather, it reveals only the broad trends and patterns that policy may be based upon—to shade that information, the personal accounts of constituents become necessary.

There are a lot of moving pieces in macroeconomics in order to consider how well a country is doing on a national scale, but this information gives you some insight into the big picture of our economy. By now, you should be able to see how important economic policy is to the prosperity we all want to achieve, both as a nation and as individuals. It is important to understand the basic building blocks of economics so that you can evaluate the economic policies our representatives want to put in place. If they are not implementing good, smart policy, it will affect you, your pocketbook, your opportunities, and our country's ability to grow.

CHAPTER 9

Let's Get Fiscal!
All About Fiscal Policy

Fiscal policy refers to government policies for taxing (revenue collection) and spending (the decisions by Congress and the presidential administration that divvy up the revenue). While this may seem simple, it is very complex in practice. Fiscal policy is full of incentives, disincentives, and practices that are intended to help the economy, but the unintended consequences and unseen effects are often much different from what was intended.

Understanding how the economy functions and grows is the key to good fiscal management. But when the public does not look at the economic implications of proposed tax/spend policies, bad policy and poor outcomes are bound to occur. This sentiment is consistent with what Alexis de Tocqueville, the French philosopher, said in the early 1800s: "The American Republic will endure until politicians realize they can bribe people with their own money."[1] Politicians have learned that to be elected, they can "bribe people with their own money." Heavy taxation, or borrowing, to "give" money to the electorate is not good policy, but it may get politicians elected and re-elected.

. . . .

"When you want to help people, tell them the truth; when you
want to help yourself, tell them what they want to hear."
—Economist Thomas Sowell[2]

. . . .

Federal Budget Basics

The federal government collects and spends trillions of dollars per year. Most people probably don't have any idea where the government gets all that money nor how it is spent. First, let's look at how and from where the government collects revenue.

The vast amount of federal revenue is collected from individuals' earnings. Individual income taxes accounted for almost half of revenue in 2020, while payroll taxes to fund Medicare and the Social Security system accounted for another 38 percent. Corporate income taxes and other taxes on goods and estates accounted, respectively, for about 8.5 and 6.2 percent of federal revenue.[3]

Because federal taxes are based mostly on earnings, the federal tax system is very progressive. Under a progressive tax system, effective tax rates (taxes as a percent of income) rise along with a person's income. As shown in Figure 9.1 below, the average person in the lowest two quintiles pays a negative effective tax rate because of various tax credits for lower-income households. For the top 1 percent of earners, about 29 percent of income goes to the federal government, and about 30 percent of income is collected from the top .1 percent of our earners.[4]

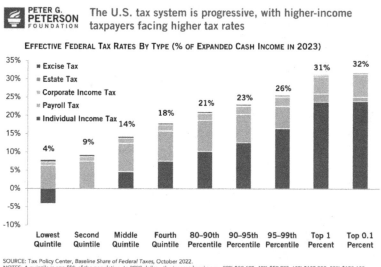

Figure 9.1. Tax rates are graphed to represent the effective tax rate for varying income quintiles.

So now that we know how and where the revenue comes from, let's review how it's generally spent, using our current history as a guide. In 2020, the federal government collected $3.4 trillion and spent $6.6 trillion, meaning that it had a budget deficit of about $3.2 trillion. A large portion of that deficit was from a burst of spending to deal with the COVID-19 pandemic, but large deficits have been the norm for years. The graphic below (Figure 9.2) illustrates this time period breaking spending into mandatory spending, discretionary spending, and net interest. **Mandatory spending** is for benefit programs with spending levels determined by existing laws. The spending is called mandatory because it would take a change in laws to adjust the spending levels or the benefits people get. **Discretionary spending** is spending that is determined each year through the budget process. The largest single category of discretionary spending is on defense, which accounted for just under 11 percent of federal spending. Nondefense discretionary spending includes money for transportation, housing assistance, education, and other programs. **Net interest** is the interest paid on funds borrowed to pay for past deficits.[5]

Revenues, $3.4 Trillion

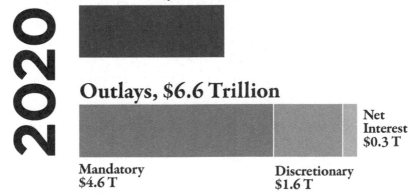

Figure 9.2. Two bars show the amount of money collected by the government (revenue) versus the amount the government spent (outlays) in 2020. The outlays bar nearly doubles the revenue bar, illustrating a budget deficit.

As shown in the graphic below (Figure 9.3), the three largest categories of mandatory spending are Social Security, Medicare (health insurance for seniors), and Medicaid (health insurance for low-income people).

Together they accounted for about 35 percent of all federal spending in 2020. In contrast, the share of federal spending going to national defense was less than 11 percent.[6]

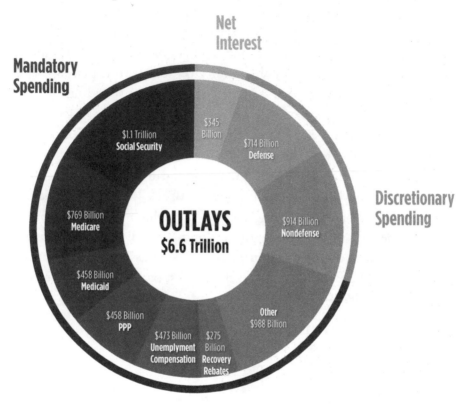

Figure 9.3. The government's outlays are broken down into categories. A second circle on the outside is shaded in three gray-scale colors for mandatory spending (dark gray), discretionary spending (medium gray), and net interest (light gray). Mandatory spending takes up a majority of funds.

Federal Deficits and Growing the Economy

Federal budget deficits have been a regular outcome for the past twenty years. As shown in Figure 9.4 below, the main source of increasing deficits will be increasing spending, not decreases in tax revenue. Without significant spending reforms, federal spending is expected to rise to over 30 percent of GDP and the annual budget deficit is expected to rise to more than 15 percent of GDP.[7]

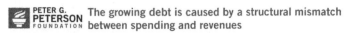

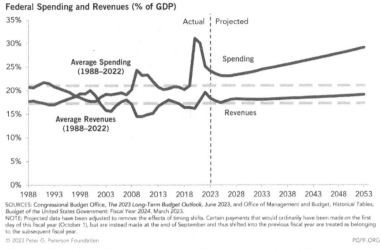

Figure 9.4. Projected federal spending is graphed alongside projected federal revenue.

The sources of the growing budget deficit are spending on Social Security and major health programs along with rising interest on federal debt. Social Security and health programs will become increasingly expensive as the average American gets older.

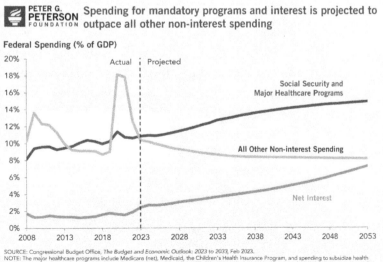

Figure 9.5. Projected spending for mandatory programs is graphed alongside projected non-interest spending.

This will combine with the interest on the debt, which will only keep rising because a) government borrowing will have to expand to finance annual deficits, and b) interest rates have been very low but will rise after the economy recovers after the pandemic of 2020–2021.

. . . .

"I contend that for a nation to try to tax itself into
prosperity is like a man standing in a bucket and
trying to lift himself up by the handle."
—WINSTON CHURCHILL (1874–1965)[8]

. . . .

When we "tax and spend," we are trying to encourage consumption to grow the economy. But is there any more output to spend it on? No, there isn't. We cannot consume what we have not produced. To grow the economy, we need to produce more, and to produce more we must have private capital investment. The more government takes, the less capital we have available to invest in productive assets. Good fiscal policy must focus on growth in production first.

Output and the standard of living for all grows with saving and investment in productive assets. This will lead to more jobs and income for consumption, thus raising the standard of living for all. When we take money out of the private economy to redistribute it, we are reducing the capital needed to invest in productive assets. It is important to look at the macroeconomics effects on the economy to evolve good policy.

> **Here's a KISSE:**
>
> TAX AND SPEND = SLOW GROWTH
>
> SAVE AND INVEST = HIGH GROWTH

Keynesian Economics

John Maynard Keynes developed a theory which was covered in his book *The General Theory of Employment, Interest and Money*, published in 1936 during the Depression.[9] In it, his basic theory was that in slow times, you could stimulate the economy via fiscal policy by "priming the pump." This means the government would spend more in the economy to put more money into it to stimulate demand, or it could cut taxes to do the same thing. During slow periods, the government would run a deficit and borrow to cover this shortfall, and in good times the government would run a surplus and would pay off the debt when spending declined and income rose.

The problem with "priming the pump" is that the government must get the money from somewhere, and when they borrow money from the public, it does not increase the economy, it only shifts things around. If money is just printed, it results in inflation, not more real output. You may have more money, but you are consuming the same amount, just at higher prices.

In practice, this has not worked. Hoover tried this in his term as president from 1929–1933. He had a surplus in 1929 when he entered office and a large deficit in 1933. Results: growth went down, and unemployment went up. Roosevelt's efforts during the Depression were no better. In fact, the Depression continued for much longer than the typical economic downturn in the economy because of this "priming the pump" approach. There are many more examples of where this approach has not worked and none where it has worked.

As core spending increases and continues, it is not justified even on Keynesian grounds. Spend and the deficit will rise not because the economy needs a boost, but because social programs expand automatically. Keynesian economics supports government deficits in the short run to get the economy out of recessions, but it does not support never-ending expansions of spending.

—$$$—

Here's a personal way to look at current fiscal policy and its future impact on us.

Based on 2020 Figures

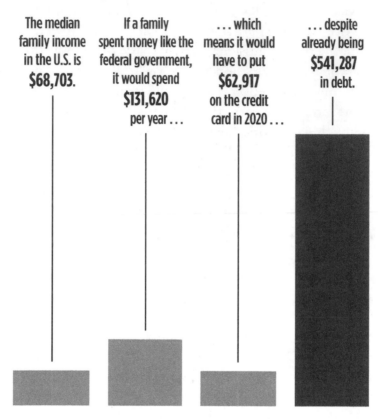

The median family income in the U.S. is **$68,703**.

If a family spent money like the federal government, it would spend **$131,620** per year . . .

. . . which means it would have to put **$62,917** on the credit card in 2020 . . .

. . . despite already being **$541,287** in debt.

Figure 9.6. If a median-income American family spent money like the U.S. government, it would have spent all of its earnings and then put nearly $63,000 on the credit card in 2020 even though it was already $541,000 in debt.

The money borrowed today to pay for the government expenses must be paid back in the future from surpluses. But there are no surpluses forecast for the next ten years, only deficits, and these deficits increase the debts and burden on the future.

The US debt as of September 2022 looked like this:

- financial statement liabilities: $39.0 trillion dollars
- unfunded Social Security + Medicare obligations: $75.9 trillion dollars
- debt owed to various government trust funds: $ 6.7 trillion dollars
- total: $121.6 trillion dollars

As of 2022, your personal share of the United States debt is $368,000, and this number will continue to rise![10] Do you have that kind of coin sitting in your pocket? Probably not.

Our current fiscal path is *unsustainable*, according to the US financials published by the Department of the Treasury, which means if we don't change the current fiscal path we are on, there will be serious economic consequences in our future!

CHAPTER 10

What the Heck Is Monetary Policy?

Monetary policy refers to the actions the Federal Reserve System (the Fed) takes to achieve the macroeconomic objectives of price stability, full employment, and stable economic growth. The federal government created the Fed in 1913 to make the national economy safer and more stable. In terms of monetary policy, the Fed's job is to pursue "price stability and maximum sustainable employment." In practice, the Fed has tried to keep inflation at about 2 percent per year while trying to keep the unemployment rate at its "natural rate." The **natural rate** is the level of unemployment when inflation is stable and GDP is at its highest possible level. The natural rate is generally thought to be between 4–5 percent.

The Fed

Despite what you may think, the Fed is not a government agency, is not funded by the government, and does not directly answer to the government. Its policies are determined by a Federal Open Markets Committee (FOMC) made up of the presidents of the twelve independent regional Feds, which spread across the country, and the seven members of the Board of Governors (based in Washington, DC). This independence guards against the Fed being used for political purposes.

The Fed pursues those two goals—price stability and maximum sustainable employment—by trying to control the economy's **money supply**. The money supply is the total of cash in circulation plus all funds that can be used for spending, such as checking accounts. The Fed has a tricky job because it must balance two goals that, sometimes, might conflict with one another. An increase in the money supply could lead to more spending on goods and services, thereby lowering the unemployment rate. On the other hand, increasing the money supply too much could lead to inflation if the money supply grew faster than the output. The job is made even trickier by the fact that the Fed doesn't really know the level of the natural unemployment rate. In addition, the natural rate is also believed to change over time from the 4–5 percent mentioned above.

Expansionary monetary policy is shown in the chart below. If the Fed thinks that the unemployment rate is too high, and it wants to promote full employment, it will buy Treasury securities from banks. These purchases provide banks with funds to lend to businesses looking to expand, consumers looking to buy cars or houses, and so on. This extra borrowing and spending should increase the money supply, boost the economy, and lower the unemployment rate. If the Fed is instead worried about inflation it would do the reverse of what is shown in Figure 10.1.

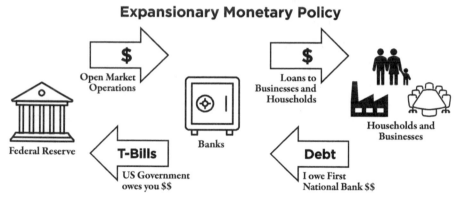

Figure 10.1. The circular flow of money starts at the federal reserve (left), through banks (center), and onto families and businesses (right). Debt and bills are then pushed through the bank back to the Fed.

The Fed's most important policy tool is open market operations: buying and selling financial assets in the open market. Prior to the 2008 financial crisis, open market operations were limited to the federal funds market, where banks borrow and lend amongst themselves to meet very short-term needs. The Fed would buy and sell in this market as an indirect way to change interest rates and the money supply.

In late 2008, the financial crisis hit and the Fed worried that the financial system might collapse and take the economy with it. Rather than work through the federal funds market, the Fed began to buy and sell financial assets directly. Many financial assets traded by the Fed are US Treasury securities. These securities include Treasury bills (T-bills), Treasury bonds, Treasury notes, and the savings bonds you might have gotten when you were a kid.

Remember that when the Fed does open market operations, it doesn't pay the banks with cash or other assets. Instead, the banks' accounts at the Fed are simply credited by the amount of the purchase. This action increases the **monetary base**, which is the amount of cash in circulation plus the reserves that banks hold at the Fed. By expanding the monetary base this way, the Fed creates money simply by entering numbers into an accounting ledger. At the same time, it is increasing the assets owned by the Fed.

The chart below (Figure 10.2) shows the annual growth of the monetary base since 1960. You can see the use of direct open market operations during and after the Great Recession and in responding to the COVID-19 pandemic during 2020–2021.

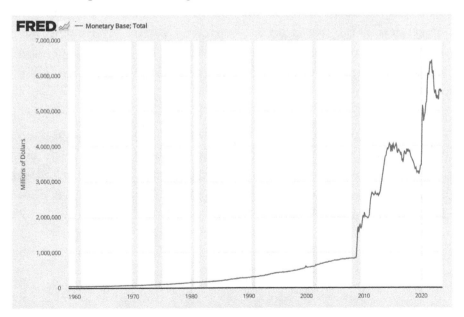

Sources: Data from Board of Governors of the Federal Reserve System (2023); Image from FRED, Federal Reserve Bank of St. Louis (2023).

Figure 10.2. The annual growth of the US's total monetary base is graphed from 1960 onwards, reflected alongside periods of recession shaded in gray.

Another key policy tool is **interest rates**. The Fed set the federal funds interest rate through the Federal Open Market Committee, which is the rate that banks borrow or lend to other banks. **Federal funds** are excess reserves that banks have that are deposited in the Federal Reserve Banks. Any increases to this rate cause all rates to increase, which tends to slow the economy by making borrowing costs more expensive. For instance, higher home mortgage interest rates slow down home construction which causes delays in many businesses related to building homes. Lowering rates, as you might imagine, has the opposite effect. Interest rates were held very low (near zero) until 2022. This, along with major increases in the money supply in 2020 and 2021, caused rapid inflation starting in 2021. So, the Fed policy in 2022 is to raise the federal funds rate to slow the growth in the money supply and combat inflation.

Financing the Deficit and Printing Money

Fiscal and monetary policy in the United States have usually operated independently. The reason for this separation is that governments have often resorted to "printing money" to cover the government's spending. Doing so can be very dangerous for the economy and has often led to hyperinflation.

Sometimes money printing is meant literally: paper currency would be printed and given to the government to spend. Not all money is paper, however, so modern money printing can occur when the government borrows directly from the central bank. It's important to know that it is illegal for the Fed to lend directly to the federal government. But if it were possible, it would look like Figure 10.3 below.

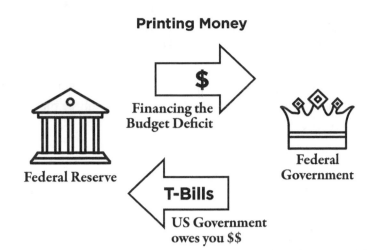

Figure 10.3. A conceptual concept of what lending between the federal reserve and the federal government would look like.

The federal government creates T-bills or other securities and sells them to the Fed, which then credits the government's account at the Fed.

In an era with expansionary monetary policy and rising budget deficits, monetary and fiscal policy in the US have become linked. As shown in Figure 10.3, the Fed has, in effect, been printing money to finance the federal deficit. The federal government finances its deficit by selling T-bills to banks. To keep encouraging lending to the public, the Fed will buy T-bills from the banks, thus increasing the banks' liquidity and desire to lend. Intentionally or not, the Fed is printing money indirectly by financing the government deficit through its open market operations. Banks serve as the Fed's middlemen in dealing with the federal government.

When the federal government runs a fiscal deficit, it must finance the short fall by one of three ways:

1. raise additional revenue through taxation to eliminate or reduce the deficit;
2. borrow from the public or private institutions to finance the deficit, if any; or
3. "borrow" from the Fed (indirectly, but this is the effect) to finance the deficit, which is in reality printing money.

When the government runs a deficit, it is, by definition, putting more money into the economy than it takes out through taxation. If it borrows from the public or private sector, it is taking money back out of the economy. The result is an even offset. There is no effect on the money supply. Now, if it "borrows" from the Fed, there is new money created in the economy and the money supply is increased. If the money supply increases faster than the output of goods and services, prices will be bid up (supply and demand curves) and create inflation.

CHAPTER 11

How International Trade Makes the World Go Round

International trade is simply the trade between countries of the world. But why do we trade? Is it good or bad? Do large trade deficits hurt our economy? Is a "strong dollar" good? Is a "weak dollar" bad? There's a lot of questions when it comes to international trade, and in this chapter, I'll provide you with answers.

Comparative Advantage

Fundamental to understanding why we trade is the concept of **comparative advantage.** This was explained in Chapter 4, but for a quick review, every country has certain advantages and disadvantages to their economy relative to other countries. Some are more efficient at producing certain goods and less so with other goods. A country's total output is maximized by using the most efficient producers of goods and services available to them. For example, China's comparative advantage is based on low labor costs, so there are many things they can make more cheaply than we can. Most US consumers will buy the cheaper imported goods rather than the more expensive US-manufactured goods. But the US has advantages of its own. We have large industries which require major capital investment, such as aircraft manufacturing. Many foreign countries do not have our infrastructure and cannot produce large aircraft, so they will buy them from the countries, like the US, that can produce them.

Sometimes comparative advantage arises because of raw materials, such as oil, being relatively abundant in one or more countries. Other countries will buy from those with an abundance of raw materials.

Free trade among countries' businesses and consumers occurs when both parties have a benefit from the exchange. One needs the product or raw material while the other will want the money, which will generate a profit or satisfaction for them.

Strong Dollar versus Weak Dollar

Currencies are freely traded between countries today. The exchange rate is the ratio of what a given currency will buy for another currency. From the perspective of the US, exchange rates are usually stated in terms of how many units of a foreign currency you can buy with a dollar. Say that today the yen/dollar exchange rate is 112.8 and you brought a dollar to a Japanese bank—they would give you 112.8 yen for it.

Exchange rates vary day to day based on the supply and demand for each currency. This is influenced by many factors, such as the amount of goods and services that countries trade with one another, the amount of foreign investment between countries, and the monetary policies of the countries. Governments often try to manipulate their exchange rates to obtain some trading advantage.

When a currency becomes "stronger" it will buy more of another currency than it formerly could, and its exchange rates will fall. A yen/dollar exchange rate of 120 would mean a stronger dollar and a weaker yen compared to the prior example. It also means that our dollars can buy more goods from Japan than before, which is good for US consumers. On the other hand, a stronger dollar is the same as a weaker yen, so US goods will be more expensive to Japanese consumers, which is bad for US exporters.

Trade Deficits and the Balance of Trade

The US carries a large trade deficit every year that amounts to hundreds of billions of dollars. This situation is often thought of as an "unfavorable balance of trade." A trade deficit is even seen as an indicator that we are losing to the rest of the world when it comes to trade. In 2020, the value of goods and services that American residents and firms bought from sellers overseas was $679 billion higher than what non-American residents and firms bought from sellers in the US.

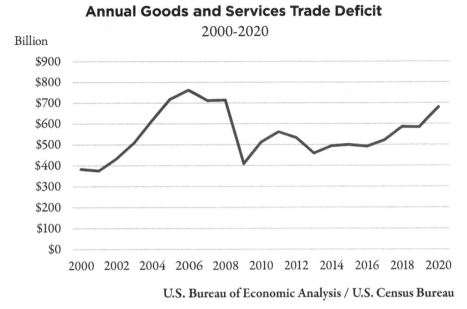

Figure 11.1 A steady incline from the early two thousands was met with a sharp decline in 2008. Since then, the deficit has slows risen back up to near 2005 numbers.

What would happen if people in the rest of the world sold more to us than we sell to them? All these trades in goods and services leave the world with more US dollars in the hands of foreigners, but these extra dollars are not buried in a hole. They are used to buy assets in the US. Overseas investors will invest in US firms, buy US Treasury debt, build factories in the US, and so on. The US is a relatively good and safe place to invest in, and this foreign investment creates jobs, income, and wealth for Americans.

Our standard of living is improved by having more goods and services, not by having more money. We maximize our standard of living with free trade, getting the most for our money. This is the result of buying the lowest-cost products from the most efficient producers. Trade might harm some industries while being beneficial to others, but the total effect is positive and a higher output and GDP.

Therefore, a more complete picture considers these capital flows into the US alongside the flows of goods and services that make up the trade deficit. In fact, the flows in and out of the US tend to exactly balance out in the foreign exchange market. Put another way, the trade deficit that so many people worry about is not a measure of winning or losing at trade.

All trade is mutually beneficial, so it's win-win. And the more trade, the better.

International Trade Interferences

International trade is like any other voluntary trade between two parties; it's just one that facilitates the ability of all countries to improve their standard of living. Why is that? There are three reasons:

1. **Each country has its unique "comparative advantage."** Some are positioned to produce certain items cheaper than other countries. When we can buy from other countries cheaper than we can produce it ourselves, then we will trade our money for their product. Then our factors of production can be used for other things that we do better or more efficiently. We can get more goods for the same money and increase our standard of living.
2. **By concentrating our resources, we can achieve economies of scale and lower the cost of production.** This means we can sell cheaper, and all can have more goods for the same money both domestically and internationally.
3. **International trade promotes competition in domestic markets**. This will lower prices and provide more goods for the same money while improving the standard of living.

But despite the near universal agreement among economists that international trade is a good thing, and that a trade deficit is irrelevant, governments around the world frequently try to interfere with it. Interference with international trade can take many forms:

1. **Tariffs:** taxes on imported goods
2. **Quotas:** limits on imports
3. **Exchange-rate manipulation:** artificially holding down the value of domestic currency to encourage exports/discourage imports
4. **Regulations**

Interference of all types holds down the gains obtained by free trade. Yet they are commonplace as countries try to encourage certain actions through their policies. For example, the "buy American" theme is promoted by some politicians, and to make this meaningful to the consumers/voting public, they might put tariffs/quotas on certain items to protect some industry, which often has well-organized groups with lobbying capabilities. Industries and lobbying groups influence politicians to make policies for their benefit. The trade-off is that good and sound economics are overruled by political expediency. Some believe this will protect jobs and benefit an industry. It may help a particular industry but at a cost to the entire economy. These interferences do not protect jobs in an economy, but rather reshuffle them. The net result is that inefficiencies occur when we are not able to buy from the most efficient producers.

The Smoot-Hawley Tariff Act is a famous and devastating example of this lack of understanding of international trade. In 1930, Congress passed the Smoot-Hawley trade bill, which allowed for dramatic increases in tariffs. The goal was to protect US producers, stimulate the economy, and reduce unemployment. Other countries responded in kind, and international trade plunged as a result; so too did output in the US. Tariff revenue declined, the benefits from trade were lost, GDP plunged, and the unemployment rate went from 8.7 percent to 23.6 percent.[1] Many economists warned President Hoover, but to no avail. The bill was a major factor, among many, that deepened and lengthened the Great Depression.

—$$$—

Free trade, especially international trade, increases the standard of living for all countries. Remember, our standard of living is determined by the goods and services we consume for the least amount of money. It is not the number of jobs we create or save; it is the impact on the overall economy. The US has grown to be the most prosperous country in the world with trade deficits. This is not harmful to the economy, and we should strive for free trade to enhance our standard of living. To the extent that we interfere with international trade and have less efficient use of resources, the standard of living is impaired.

PART TWO
REVIEW OF OUR MAJOR ISSUES

CHAPTER 12

A Funny Thing Happened on the Way to Broke

This country is broke and broken. I'm sorry to be the bearer of bad news, but it is true. If you truly reflect on how the United States was started and how it got to be the Greatest of All Time, then look at where our country is today and where it's headed, and you'll be able to see it even with blinders on. I know our history is not perfect, but it started from a group of liberty-seeking individuals with great wisdom and leadership. They were statesmen, not politicians, who wanted to do the right thing for this fledgling country. They threw off the yoke of British and big government oppression and became free in their thought and actions with limited government intervention. And as Thomas Jefferson wrote in the Declaration of Independence:

. . . .

"We hold these truths to be self-evident, that all men are
created equal, that they are endowed by their Creator with
certain unalienable Rights, that among these are Life, Liberty,
and the pursuit of Happiness. That to secure these rights,
Governments are instituted among Men, deriving their just
powers from the consent of the governed . . ."
—THE DECLARATION OF INDEPENDENCE[1]

. . . .

In that spirit, they developed the most thoughtful Constitution that has stood the test of time. It detailed what government is and what its role should be. All else was left to the people or states. The Preamble to our Constitution sums this ideal up perfectly.

· ·

"We the People of the United States, in Order to form
a more perfect Union, establish Justice, ensure domestic
Tranquility, provide for the common defense, promote
the general Welfare, and secure the Blessings of Liberty to
ourselves and our Posterity, do ordain and establish this
Constitution for the United States of America."
—THE PREAMBLE TO THE US CONSTITUTION[2]

· ·

Our Founding Fathers' intellect and skills in developing the political
and economic system we have is nothing short of remarkable. It is
based on incentives and ideas from great thinkers like Adam Smith,
who understood human nature as well as economics. In *An Inquiry
into the Nature and Causes of the Wealth of Nations*,[3] Smith explained
that individuals would benefit themselves, as well as others, if they
were left to pursue what was in their best interest and their rights
to life, liberty, and property were secure and protected.[3] This is his
concept of the "Invisible Hand" of self-interest which provides the
incentives that propel us. The government's job would be to provide for
these protections. We have become the wealthiest nation with the highest
standard of living across the general population in the world because
of these ideas.

Unfortunately, the United States and its economy has drifted off
course. Government has expanded far beyond what was envisioned by our
Founding Fathers. The Founding Fathers were statesmen, whose interests
were focused on what was best for the new nation. Today, the politicians'
main focus seems to be on getting re-elected, so they choose laws, regulations, and policies to get the most votes and/or contributions. They ignore
or push into the background what is in the best interests of the citizens at
large.

Rules, regulations, and government programs have grown beyond
comprehension. Elected officials and policymakers do things that "look
good but feel bad." They make promises where no one is held accountable
for whether they successfully achieve their desired outcomes. They ignore
the unintended consequences of new laws, rules, and regulations as well as

the impact they have on all the general citizens, including those living in poverty or minority households.

Today, government spending and debt are out of control. Borrowing to meet obligations and keep unfunded promises while taking on debt that is unlikely to be repaid? It's all reckless. This places our future in jeopardy. We are mortgaging the future of our kids and grandkids for today's fleeting benefit.

Are you comfortable with all of this? Consider how it affects you and your daily life. Just take a few minutes to think about how government affects your life. Consider the proliferation of the rules, regulations, (unsound) programs, and taxes around you. Has government gone beyond its intended purpose? Are the programs well thought out enough to get the intended results? Is the government held accountable for results, both good and bad? Is it doing more harm than good? Maybe you don't see or know this in full yet, but you will soon. As you read on, you'll understand how the costs of government have exceeded the benefits and what we the people can do about it.

Maybe the biggest question on the tip of your tongue is how do we turn things around? First, we must see the problem. We must know its scope and magnitude if we are going to realize that it must be fixed and know how to fix it. Next, we'll search for feasible solutions that lead the government to return to its intended roll. Finally, we'll ask our government to act and step back before pushing us over the fiscal cliff. How do we ask? You voice your opinions to your representatives, and if they don't get it, then vote for someone who does.

"Relax! Have I steered you wrong before?"

CHAPTER 13

The Rising Federal Debt:
Where Are We and How Did We Get Here?

The 2022 US Treasury annual reports states that the "current fiscal path is unsustainable," which means we are headed over the fiscal cliff if government policy remains on its current course![1]

· ·

"If current policy is left unchanged and based on this report's assumptions, the debt-to-GDP ratio is projected to exceed 200 percent by 2041 and reach 700 percent in 2096. Preventing the debt-to-GDP ratio from rising over the next 75 years is estimated to require some combination of spending reductions and revenue increases that amount to -2 percent of GDP over the period."
—THE 2022 US TREASURY ANNUAL REPORT[2]

· ·

This is not a personal observation. The US government has "fessed up" and published this clear warning in its financial statements.

While this estimate of the "seventy-five-year fiscal gap" is highly uncertain, it is nevertheless nearly certain that current fiscal policies cannot be sustained indefinitely. So we must ask, "Where are we and how did we get here?"

The following table (Figure 13.1) summarizes the current debts and unfunded obligations as of September 30, 2022, the most recent financials produced by the Department of the Treasury:

	2021	2022
Financial statement liabilities	$34.80	$39.02
Unfunded Social Security and Medicare obligations	$71.00	$75.90
Debt owed to various government trust funds	$6.20	$6.70
Total	$112.00	$121.62

*The numbers in this chart are in the trillions of dollars.[3]

Figure 13.1. Table shows the change in liabilities, Social Security and Medicare obligations, and debt to trust funds between 2021 and 2022—a difference of $9.62 trillion.

The financial statement liabilities of $39.02 trillion includes $24.7 trillion of federal interest-bearing debt (which is found in the financial statements of the federal government), with another $6.7 trillion of interest-bearing debt owed to the government trust funds (which are not counted in the total liabilities for some unknown reason) for a total of $31.4 trillion and keeps growing. The unfunded obligations are future payments promised for entitlement programs, for which there is no funding planned or available.[4]

From 1960 to 2008, the federal debt—as related to the size of the economy (GDP)—remained between 30 percent and 65 percent of GDP. Since 2008 it has exploded to almost 130 percent of GDP and growing fast as Figure 13.2 reveals and Figure 13.3 illustrates the debt to GDP.[5]

If fiscal spending and tax policies remain unchanged, the US federal debt is projected to exceed 700 percent of GDP within eighty years. This is not sustainable and will destroy our economy and country if we let this trend continue.

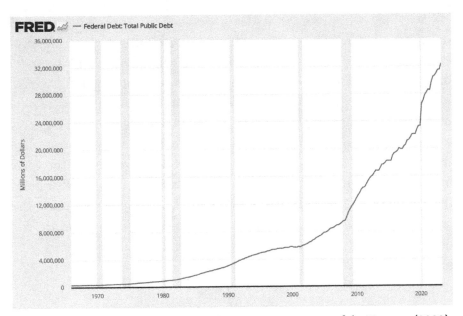

**Sources: Data from U.S. Department of the Treasury (2023);
Image from FRED, Federal Reserve Bank of St. Louis (2023)."**

Figure 13.2. The upward trend of public debt is graphed from 1970 onwards.

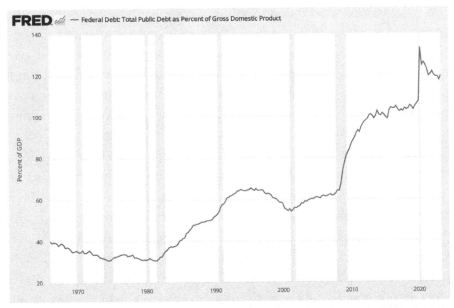

**Sources: Data from U.S. Office of Management and Budget and FRED (2023);
Image from Federal Reserve Bank of St. Louis FRED (2023).**

Figure 13.3. The public debt as related to the GDP climbed dramatically over recent decades.

We got here by promising to do things for people that we did not, and could not, pay for. Many were outside the primary function of federal government, which is supposed to provide national defense, administration of justice, and provision of certain public goods (as outlined in Chapter 7); nowadays, the federal government is in charge of things that were supposed to be left up to the state government or individuals, like energy and education. Most of the time the intended benefits never materialized, but we continued to do them anyway. And we do not pay for them. There has been no responsible budgeting and control of our fiscal policies for more than sixty years. During this period there have been only three years in the late 1990s in which we had a balanced budget or surplus. Even worse, the unsustainable path we are already on doesn't include the many new programs proposed. Yes, it can get even worse.

The Debt Bomb Is Ticking!

At first glance, the deficit seems like a simple math problem. Why can't we just save rather than deficit spend? It seems that the government can simply collect more revenue and reduce spending. But it isn't that simple. Instead of being a simple math problem, there are complexities to consider. Deciding where to spend less in current programs or who will pay more in taxes makes things extremely complicated. Nevertheless, it must be done. To avoid the dreadful consequences of mass starvation and economic collapse, some combination of spending reductions and revenue increases are necessary. If not, we will fall off the fiscal cliff.

Yes, Congress and the President (no matter who holds the position) have hard decisions in front of them. Analyzing the net impact of changing the landscape of public and social policy is complicated. There are many layers and forces at play. To bring everything together and provide a concrete solution is impossible for one person, one group, or one Congress and President. However, a commitment to reverse the current policy course can be made. We, as a country, must demand that they get to work and reverse the course of the US economy by returning government to doing what it should do and what it does best: protecting our lives and liberties while supplying a few public goods such as protecting our borders and supporting a fair judicial system. Forget everything else.

There are a few main actions we can take right now to help avoid this ticking debt bomb:

1. **Learn economics!** Know what works and what doesn't work. Spend less than you earn or receive in revenue. Use what remains to save and invest productively. Profitable businesses do it. Financially secure individuals and families do it. Ask Congress and the President to do it. Help make the US solvent and sustainable.

2. **Vote smart!** We must recognize that long-term prosperity is at risk. Commit your vote to doing something about it. Continue to educate yourself and others on these matters. Encourage meaningful discussion on ways to reduce government spending, raise tax revenues through wealth-enhancing activities, and shift government resources into public savings and investment. Act and move the dial toward focusing on what government does best. Let the individuals living in households and running businesses do the rest.

3. **Take action!** Express your opinions to your representatives. If they don't get it, then vote for someone who does.

4. **Pay attention!** If you are not seeing the problem, then you are not looking at the facts. This problem is too big to ignore. And if we do ignore it, it's at our own peril.

"I just don't understand why your business isn't more successful."

CHAPTER 14

Government Interference in the Marketplace

In our country, we are a nation of laws which govern a civilized society. We are also a market economy where free enterprise and open markets are the norm. This form of economic-government relationship works best as we all pursue what is in our best interest, and it is in the best interest of businesses to please customers if they desire success. After all, businesses are only successful if they can sell their products at a profit to customers willing and able to pay for them. Their whole reason for being is to please someone else to make a profit.

This system works well if the government has reasonable laws, rules, and regulations appropriate to its purpose. Why? Because you need peace to prosper. However, burdensome regulations and interference in the marketplace disrupts the smooth operation of a market economy. This can cause imbalances and extraordinary costs which are counterproductive, benefiting a few at the cost of many.

There are 188,000 pages in the Code of Federal Regulations. It has increased by 175 percent since 1975 and the current administration is making it longer by the minute. They are proposing an additional 2,673 rules over the next 12 months. Of these, 217 actions are considered "major," which means each major regulation costs more than $100 million to implement. And most are extraordinary overreach with potentially little or no benefits, and they haven't conducted analysis to see if what they are implementing is beneficial to businesses. They just get created from an unaccountable bureaucracy.[1]

One study done several years ago estimated that if regulations were held at 1980 levels in 2012, our economy would have been 25 percent larger with GDP growing at .8 percent faster per year. In 2012, incomes would have averaged $13,000 higher per person.[2] Our current "red tape" and regulations cost many billions of hours of wasted effort and trillions of dollars in cost. This makes it hard for small businesses to succeed, causing more concentration in big business.

For instance, Jesse, president of a minority and veteran-owned business consulting group in Louisiana, says that he faces difficulty navigating the unclear federal laws on what constitutes an employee and what constitutes an independent contractor.[3] Using independent contractors is crucial to his business, which must remain flexible to meet the demands of diverse clients and tasks. However, there are penalties for misclassifying employees, which impedes the hiring process and deters business growth. Instead of focusing on providing value to customers, business owners like Jesse must allocate scarce time, money, and personnel to navigating the minefield of regulations, which makes it harder to grow and expand his company to the level he desires. These hard-to-navigate regulations and allocations of funds make him question if his business will succeed and if he should've started it in the first place.

Employee classification regulations compose just one small node on the complex web of federal regulations. Another such case is a fifth-generation apple orchard operation in New York, owned by the Tennyson family. Their work was interrupted by federal investigators during peak harvest season. The investigators interrogated their employees and requested twenty-two types of paperwork for review like vehicle registrations, insurance documents, and time sheets.[4] The small office staff was forced to turn its attention away from commerce to defend their operation. With rules on pesticides alone running over ten thousand words, the owners were expected to be proficient in thirty-three legally precise definitions, including a forty-five-word description of the word "hazard." This is not to mention the pages of regulations on ladders, hygiene, immigrant workers, storage, fertilizers, and more. In all, the disruptive visits cost Mr. Tennyson and his farm forty hours' worth of work. Though suffering a loss of time and money had taken a bat to his margins, this is a small cost compared to some other farmers, who have lost their land, homes, and livelihood having to keep up with the increasing amount of regulations, which grow stricter each year.

Although Mr. Tennyson may have managed to jump through the hoops this time around, it certainly came at a cost. Not only the financial

GOVERNMENT INTERFERENCE IN THE MARKETPLACE

loss but also the psychological anxiety of being inspected for a fine. There has been increasing new food and safety regulations over the past five decades that Mr. Tennyson has been in business, and he anticipates only more regulatory control. Ever-expanding federal regulations are costly and debilitating for small businesses and ultimately result in them falling behind larger corporations.[5]

Our Issues Specifically

Here are some of the issues from the government that cause problems:

- **Burdensome regulations.** There are rules and regulations appropriate for managing an economy, but when these regulations go beyond what is needed, it causes various problems. For example, starting a new business often requires a license. The purpose of licensing is to protect the public. But does every business need a license? And how complex and costly does the process have to be? Instances of unnecessary licenses or extraordinary cost, processes, and delays instituted by the government or their unelected bureaucracy make for totally unnecessary and very costly in time and/or money requirements.

- **Crony capitalism.** Sometimes a government wants to promote some special thing for a business or group of businesses to achieve a desired outcome. It can do this by giving government incentives to specific groups or industries when others do not get this incentive. They are using taxpayer money for the benefit of a few, at the expense of many, who might not want the taxpayer funds used like this. This is unfair cronyism. It is not the government's job to pick winners and losers but the market's.

- **Subsidies.** This is a form of cronyism where selected people or businesses get a benefit paid for by the taxpayer. For example, a purchaser of an electric vehicle (EV) will get a subsidy from buying an EV to promote a government aim regardless of whether the goal is a good one, which it is not for electric cars as it does not achieve the intended outcome of mitigating climate change and is an expense to the consumer (energy and initiatives will be further discussed in Chapter 15). The intended results are to reduce carbon emissions, but electric vehicles have a minimal impact on reducing carbon output when considering the entire life cycle of the vehicle, including mining the materials required to produce the batteries. Another subsidy may be to decide to forgive student loans in whole or part—loans that the student voluntarily took out, and the taxpayers will be paying part or all of it. Or the government may subsidize the agricultural community with price supports, which benefit a few, and we all pay for the costs when the government must buy the surpluses they created as well as higher prices for all in the market (like the farm example in Chapter 3).

- **Price controls.** From time to time, a government will see a problem with higher prices of some goods or services. To "help" those who might not be able to afford the item, it will authorize price controls to keep it affordable. Even though the intentions may be good, the results will not be. Why? Because limiting the price does not cause there to be more available; in fact, usually it will discourage production, resulting in less of the good to be available. Similarly, none could/will be produced if the price is so low business cannot produce it at a profit. This often leads to illegal black markets so the normal supply and demand pricing will be reestablished, and goods and services will be available at a market price. Rent controls are another form of this. What this does is limit the supply of rental units, which hurts those who want to find a place to live. A few benefit, but many are just out of luck.

- **Going green.** Climate change is thought, by many, that it's caused by greenhouse gases. To foster less greenhouse gases, governments have recently disincentivized production of fossil fuels in order to encourage green energy, which is more expensive. The market does not have a good solution to greenhouse gases yet, but the government thinks EVs are a solution. (Chapter 15 will discuss more in depth why EVs do very little to reduce carbon with today's technology.) To push EVs, the government discourages fossil fuels by limiting its supply. This has had the effect of driving up prices of fossil fuels and making EVs relatively more attractive. This costs the entire economy significantly due to higher prices, as we cannot do without energy in modern life. The intentions may be good, but the result is terrible for the entire economy.

—$$$—

The government may want to promote certain results by interfering in the market even if that is not the best answer for you. But when it interferes, it disrupts the market and does not get an economically good answer. This negatively affects you and most often it gets just the opposite of its intentions when considering the cost/benefits to the overall economy.

Government should look at the overall economic effects of what it plans to do and the possible unintended consequences. It will often realize that the best solution is to do nothing. Let the market work naturally as much as possible. The market will allocate scarce resources efficiently if we let it.

*"The good news is our ESG score is the best in the industry.
The bad news is the company is broke."*

CHAPTER 15

Energy Supply

Energy has been the key factor in bringing most of the world out of poverty and is now essential to everyday life. In industrialized nations, we are accustomed to flipping a switch and getting light, turning on a stove or A/C, running a factory, and using power whenever we need it—all at a reasonable price. Energy is needed for nearly everything we do. Reliable and affordable power has become the norm.

But will that continue to be the norm?

Our most popular sources of electricity production have been fossil fuels and nuclear energy, but we have a new concern called global warming. There is debate over the degree and significance of this, but most agree something is changing and it is, to some extent, the result of carbon and methane emissions generated by human activities.

Most people share the basic common goals. We all want to keep affordable energy and keep—possibly make better—a clean planet. We want better technologies that help us meet both objectives. Governments, as we saw in Chapter 14, take a step to do this with "Go Green!" initiatives and government subsidies, but these often lead to less effective results than if the market had left them alone and don't create as much impact as we'd hope. That's because the problem is not just the US's; it's the world's.

According to John Kerry, the "czar of the environment," almost 90 percent of all of the planet's global emissions comes from outside of US borders.[1] Let's take a second and put that in perspective. As Kerry acknowledges, fixing it in the US does not solve the problem. There would be negligible impact worldwide if we got to zero carbon emissions because this is a *worldwide* problem.

The Paris Accord is an international treaty on climate change intended to resolve the problem. Yes, it has the promises of the major polluters to fix things in the next decade, but those ten-year goals just never seem to happen. It's called "kicking the can down the road." Meanwhile hundreds of coal-fired power plants are being constructed *each year* in China and India.

That doesn't mean we should ignore the issue. You, me, and our country should be leaders in technology and practical solutions to move in the right direction—and we have been. Our emissions have gone down substantially over the past twenty years, and we continue to work on it. *However,* we are going to extreme and costly measures to try to be perfect (i.e., zero carbon), which will have a negligible effect on the worldwide problem.

A Commonsense Approach: Costs versus Benefits

When comparing the alternatives, the commonsense approach is to weigh the costs and benefits of each option. We need to recognize that we live in a world of unlimited desires—which in this case a perfect, pure world with no pollution or climate change and unlimited, low-cost energy for everyone—with limited resources. Each energy production option has costs and benefits. We can't just ignore the costs, and we need to take seriously the benefits. Both matter for a reasonable solution.

Some people today make emotional pleas to go "green" no matter the cost to society. But this is not helpful. It's alarmist and ignores the costs and benefits of the choices we face along with ignoring what is feasible to achieve in the short run as well. We need to act carefully and logically, not emotionally, and determine the best course of action for today that will also leave a cleaner, but realistic future for us all.

The green movement has led to policies and initiatives aimed at producing energy effectively while reducing, or even eliminating, carbon and other emissions. The most common of these utilizes the wind or the sun. Others, like the conversion of coal plants to gas, have greatly decreased emissions, but not eliminated them. Although nuclear power is "clean," there has been a long-standing taboo against its usage due to both the difficulties of disposing of nuclear waste and the fear of a nuclear accident that could release harmful radiation. As a result, it's rarely used today. Only two new nuclear plants are currently being built in the United

States, and many are being phased out even though their useful life has not yet expired.

The problem with the newer initiatives, however, is that they are not cost effective and are not yet reliable sources of energy. In the rush to get rid of fossil fuels and nuclear power in Germany, power has become scarce, leading to skyrocketing electricity costs and leaving the country dependent on gas from unreliable sources like Russia. The high costs have had unintended consequences as well, causing some people to burn wood for heating and cooking. While that's not necessarily harmful, it's never great, especially in mass quantities. Many times, these unintended consequences are now doing the opposite of what the policies originally intended, causing more harmful carbon output than before. In contrast, France has relied more heavily on nuclear energy which has allowed lower costs without the negative unintended consequences.

With today's technology, wind and sun simply cannot replace fossil fuels in producing sufficient and reliable energy for our society. They are both costly and require very large amounts of land and raw material to produce the power. While the source of energy is clean (wind or sun), they require tremendous energy and raw materials to build and require major new distribution lines to get the power to where it is needed. Further, because they are intermittent—only generating energy when the sun shines or the wind blows—they cannot fully replace the traditional forms of electrical production. Sadly, there is no practical way, so far, to store enough energy from an intermittent source to provide enough power when we need it.

Markets and competition have led to some improvements in new technologies, even in wind- and solar-power production. But the biggest gains in carbon reduction came from private developments in clean oil and gas production. (When gas replaced coal, major reductions in carbon output occurred.)[2] By 2019, new technologies called "fracking" allowed the US to become energy independent but policies since then have slowed development to become "green" faster and we are no longer producing and expanding our energy supply fast enough to meet ever increasing demands of the modern world.

These policy changes have made us increasingly dependent on other countries for gas and oil and the supply/demand imbalance has been leading to dramatically higher prices once again. The demand for energy is inelastic and goes down slowly as prices go up since we are dependent on energy and there are no readily available substitutes. That will not change, and we will only need even more energy as we grow.

The problem we face is how to balance the ever-increasing need for energy and deal with the climate effect of man-made emissions in a logical and cost-effective manner. Everyone needs both energy to live and a clean planet to live on. Technology is constantly improving, and the answers we think of today will be different tomorrow. But we must deal with today's challenges effectively while technology evolves, allowing for a more efficient and cleaner future.

Energy Supply

Over the last one hundred years, there have been dire predictions of catastrophic climate changes from an impending ice age to global warming. In recent years, there is evidence that the temperatures are rising to some degree. This could result in rising sea levels and major weather or other environmental catastrophes while, on the flip side, over the last few decades, the air quality has risen significantly. And with the discovery of fracking, much more gas has been discovered and used for electrical generation. This is a much cleaner fuel than coal, which it is often replacing. Carbon emissions have dropped appreciably. But is this enough? With today's proven technologies, what can we, and should we, do about what has not improved?

Many are advocating for zero carbon emissions, which leads to securing our electricity from sources which do not emit carbon dioxide and to power our vehicles with batteries so as not to pollute the air with carbon. Is this possible? Is it a good idea? What is the best policy for energy in this country when all factors are considered?

There are three "proven" technologies which currently produce power with no carbon emissions—wind, sun and nuclear. The predominant sources for power generation today are fossil fuels (coal, oil, and gas) and nuclear, with a clear trend toward cleaner gas-use replacing coal, which produces almost twice the carbon as gas. There are many other clean energy sources which have not been used extensively yet as they are not presently commercially viable. It is very possible some of these will become the energy source of the future, but this will not solve the needs for today.

Nuclear

Today, nuclear is the only "clean" source which has any significant amount of generation, around 20 percent of total power produced.[3] Politically, it has been a problem in our country and some other countries due to fear of accidents and concerns about waste disposal. There are only two plants under construction today in the US, and both have long delays and costly overruns. As mentioned before, many plants are closing or scheduled to phase out before their useful life has ended.

Accidents are a risk—but not a high risk compared to other types of electric-generating approaches. Consider these three high profile accidents: Three Mile Island in 1979, Chernobyl in 1986, and Fukushima in 2011. While these are concerning, the safety record of nuclear power is very good compared to other forms of energy production. Nuclear energy has resulted in almost 100 percent fewer deaths than coal and close to 98 percent less than the gas industry.[4] The nuclear waste is well-controlled by being encapsulated in steel and concrete before being buried in the desert. It takes only a small amount of land to handle all of it.

The old-style large plants are probably not the future as they have gotten very costly and difficult to permit and build. Small Modular Reactors (SMRs), an advanced type of nuclear reactor, are being developed. They can be produced in factories at likely much less expensive rates while having a speedier production time once the design is approved. There are more than sixty companies working on these, and they are all nuclear fusion, but this will take several years to get into production. Nuclear fission may be the solution, but this is not practical yet.

Examining France, Sweden, and Germany is enlightening as well. France and Sweden, which have some of the lowest per capita carbon emissions in the developed world, both rely heavily on nuclear (72 percent and 42 percent, respectively) rather than on wind or solar power. In contrast, Germany has gone away from nuclear and coal and heavily into wind and solar. Unfortunately, Germany has not dramatically reduced carbon, and their electricity costs five times more than France's.[5]

> **Recommendation:** Nuclear should be incentivized, developed, and implemented as a major part of our energy program.

Wind and Solar

These do not emit carbon dioxide as they produce power. However, they require enormous amounts of material to build the wind turbines and solar panels, and this front-loads the carbon output as a result of mining and refining the many materials, metals, and minerals used. They take vast tracts of land to produce power adequate for commercial production, and it is often difficult to find suitable locations where the public will allow this.

Other environmental problems, such as killing birds and disposing of the equipment when they need replacing, are also common with wind and solar. They are expensive to build when compared to fossil fuels for an equivalent energy production. In the last twenty years, trillions of dollars have been spent to produce less than 5 percent of our overall power generation.[6]

Most critical to consider is that the power is intermittent and cannot be produced when the sun isn't shining, or the wind isn't blowing. Since there is no practical way to store the power yet, it must be coupled with a traditional power-generation system, fossil fuel, or nuclear (more on this under Electric Vehicles below). While this may be a part of the solution, for many reasons, this is not going to be the primary solution for the foreseeable future.

> **Recommendation:** Continue to improve wind and solar technology and use them as an augmentation of other reliable power sources when practical.

Fossil Fuels

With over 60 percent of power generated through fossil fuels, this has been the major source of reliable power in this country.[7] As fracking has produced more gas reserves, and gas is the cleanest of these fuels, there has been a significant trend to replace coal with gas, and this has resulted in significant reductions in carbon emissions. With the new fracking technology, we have become the major producer of fossil fuels and achieved energy independence from other nations, as we produce more than we consume. With this increased production, oil prices were stabilized, and gasoline prices were in the mid $2 per gallon range.

The current government policy is to reduce the supply of fossil fuels, drive up the prices with reduced supplies, and make "green" energy relatively more attractive. This has worked to drive up the prices, but since there are no large-scale alternatives available today, there is continued reliance on fossil fuels. As a result, energy prices increased dramatically. This has been exacerbated by the war between Russia and Ukraine, but most of the increase occurred before the war. Over the past few years, gasoline prices average between $3 and $5, much higher than before the government started restricting supply. This will always fluctuate as supply and demand changes occur. Supply is also impacted by the actions of others, such as when the oil cartel cuts production to reduce supply and increase price. Fossil fuels will be a major part of our energy requirements for the foreseeable future until other cost-effective energy sources are available.

> **Recommendation:** Encourage production and develop liquified gas terminals to be able to supply other countries, helping to move them to less carbon-producing energy sources. As other cleaner technologies develop, reduce the use of fossil fuels as much as practical.

Electric Vehicles (EV)

Go green! It's true that when you step on the "gas" pedal to accelerate an EV, you are not creating carbon emissions. But the whole story must evolve around the full life cycle of producing and operating the automobile. It is very different from what many believe.

What makes them challenging is producing and charging the battery. With today's technology, the battery takes many metals and minerals to produce, most of which are mined in countries like Africa and China. Mining for these has very low yields; it takes about five hundred thousand pounds of mined material to make a single one-thousand-pound battery. Then you must refine the mined material to extract the metals or minerals you need; only then can you manufacture the battery. Subsequently, electricity is required to charge the battery, and inevitably the battery must be replaced during the life of the car. When the entire process is accounted for, the energy needed to do all this leaves very little improvement in the carbon footprint.

The vehicles are more expensive because of the battery and will get more expensive if demand for them increases. Why? Because demand will drive up the costs of the raw material needed as demand for the raw material increases (which will also drive up the costs of many products that use the same raw materials). As of today, there is not enough discovered material to have an all-electric vehicle fleet, not even close if you have hundreds of millions of EVs on the road. Yes, more material will be discovered as demand increases, but getting mining permits is very difficult, and time consuming in the United States, if you can get one at all. On top of that, disposing of the batteries is an even bigger environmental problem.

This does not mean that EVs are not good products; they are very nice, high-tech vehicles. But they are not the panacea our politicians espouse as the solution to our carbon emissions challenge, nor are they economical as the life cycle costs are much higher than conventional gas-powered vehicles, which make them a poor choice for consumers. There is much work being done to improve batteries and recycling the material. Over time, the dynamics of EVs will change and the future may be very different. However, we must deal with what exists today until we have practical alternatives.

Recommendation: Don't allow tax money to subsidize expensive alternatives that do little for the environment. Let the market sort out the expansion of EV markets based on the merits of the vehicles.

—$$$—

With today's technology, we have already been lowering emissions through private-market technological innovations like fracking and converting coal to gas-run generators. These are not perfect solutions to get to zero carbon emissions, but they move in the right direction in an affordable and sustainable way. Driving up the cost of fossil fuels won't solve the problem now or in the future, but it is seriously impacting inflation as energy requirements permeate the economy and drive up the cost of virtually everything.

Since we, the US, are not the main problem with carbon in the atmosphere, we should be helping other major polluters move to better solutions—such as coal-to-gas conversions until better solutions for them can be invented and implemented in those areas.

We need to encourage new technologies that may solve the problem, but that will take years to develop and implement. For now, we should be developing nuclear and expanding our fossil fuel production, especially gas and oil, and become energy independent again. Nuclear will take many years to expand significantly, but we should be proceeding with this as quickly as practical.

Other technologies will evolve and someday become practical. This might include geothermal energy, biofuels, and other technologies being developed.

Until that time, we must have practical commonsense policies that work for the technology we have today.

"I'm going grocery shopping. Do you need anything?"

CHAPTER 16

Inflation

Inflation is the constant increase in "all prices" in an economy. In small and expected doses, it's typically fine. People can plan for it and make it a stable part of their lives. Stable prices help ensure that capital markets channel investments to strategic projects, job markets are stable, and people are generally confident that today's money will be worth about the same tomorrow.

If all prices rise about 2 percent a year—the US Central Bank's target inflation rate—then businesses will likely raise their prices about 2 percent every year, their production costs will likely rise about 2 percent every year, and businesses will also likely raise wages and salaries by about 2 percent a year as well. Since the prices in the stores are generally rising similarly at 2 percent, everyone can buy the same goods and services every year.

Low and stable inflation means the value of the dollar is stable. It's worth 2 percent less every year, but it's predictable and low, and we all get 2 percent more dollars every year too, so everything balances out.[1] People and markets respond well to predictable prices, and sound policies support them.

But inflation is almost like a curse word when it gets out of control. People hear it and shudder.

Why is that?

Inflation involves an upward spiral of rising prices across the economy. Unlike a sharp spike in a single item like the price of a gallon of gas or higher rent, inflation involves increasing prices of most everything across the board. So finding cheaper substitutes is almost impossible because those substitutes rise too. If your income doesn't keep pace with inflation, it can have devastating effects. Your "real" income is declining (i.e., your actual income buys less goods and services).

Understanding the devastating effects of *unexpected* inflation is important. Inflation raises the prices of everyday goods and services, making them more expensive. And typically, incomes do not rise at the same rate as inflation, so people feel the pinch as true purchasing power declines.

Inflation is indeed one of the most cruel and regressive economic punishments there is. A wealthy person can move money into investments since their house, car, gas, and grocery bills are a smaller part of their monthly budgets. But for someone with a lower income, their house, rent, car payments, gas, and grocery bills are a huge part of their monthly budgets, and all those prices will skyrocket first. And retired people are hit the hardest because their incomes are fixed; basic living expenses are their primary budget item and, with being retired, they have no way to earn extra to help themselves out of a worsening financial situation. The higher the inflation, the more damage there is.

Left unchecked, inflation debases the currency and causes serious long-term economic problems. It's like a tax on everyone that nobody voted for. And it does the most harm for those individuals in the middle- and lower-income levels and those on fixed incomes.

What Causes Inflation?

Inflation is a monetary phenomenon. The Federal Reserve Bank of the United States controls the money supply. When the Fed buys US Treasuries, lowers rates, or reduces the reserves that banks are required to hold, it supplies banks with loanable funds they can turn around and lend to both consumers to finance spending and business to build capacity.

The money supply is controlled by the Federal Reserve. When the fiscal policy of the government runs a deficit, this must be financed in some way. There are two primary choices: sell bonds to the private sector or "sell" them to the Federal Reserve. Selling to the private sector takes money out of the private sector roughly equivalent to what the government injected into it by spending more than it took in taxes. This is not increasing the money supply and not materially affecting inflation. "Selling" bonds to the Federal Reserve is essentially printing money, growing the money supply, and to the extent it grows faster than output, inflation occurs. (The Treasury does not actually sell directly to the Federal Reserve—but this is effectively the result.)

The definition of **inflation** is an increase in the general level of prices. Inflation has been a problem for governments and central banks for centuries, and *inflation is caused by increasing the money supply faster than increasing output quantities*. Think about it this way. If you suddenly doubled the money supply and did not increase the available goods and services, there would be too many dollars chasing too few goods. In other words, people would try to buy the available goods and services with more dollars. At the old prices, there is a shortage. To buy the last few goods before shelves run bare, people would bid up prices until supply and demand balance again. But now prices are higher while the quantities of products in the economy are the same.

What History Reveals

A quick peak in US history suggests that the Fed and government could have leveraged past mistakes and lessons learned to avoid the inflationary problems of today. From the mid-1960s until the early 1980s, The US government financed the Vietnam War, and the Great Society projects took social spending in many directions without sound funding considerations or metrics to determine how to improve them. Government spending financed by increasing the money supply fueled inflation.

Data from 1961 to 1990 reveal increasing government total expenditures (blue) moved in tandem with the Consumer Price Index (red).[2] (Consumer Price Index [CPI] is a popular statistic used to determine rates of inflation.) In the late 1960s, inflation started its rise and went from under 2 percent to over 5 percent by 1970 as shown below.[3]

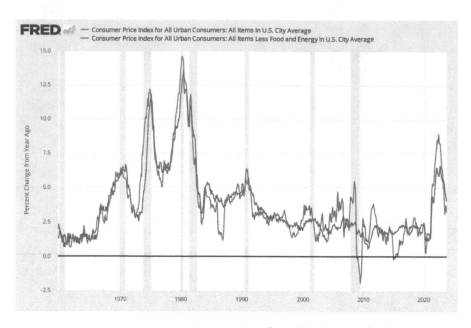

Sources: Data from U.S. Bureau of Labor Statistics;
Image from FRED, Federal Reserve Bank of St. Louis, (2023).

Figure 16.1. The Consumer Price Index for all consumer spending and all consumer spending less food and energy are graphed from the mid-to-late twentieth century onwards, illustrating the changes over time in prices paid by consumers in US cities for goods and services due to inflation.

Spending stayed high and then inflation took off as the government tried to spend its way out of economic problems, which lead to an eventual peak in inflation around 13 percent in the 1979–1981 period.[4]

Federal Reserve Chairman Paul Volcker launched a war on inflation. Through the central banking system and contractionary monetary policies, interest rates entered double digits, unemployment rose, and the economy began to reset itself. Markets emerged to flush out the negative influences of government, pushing out inefficiencies, stepping forward with sound projects, and new initiatives, returning the US to its growth trajectory.

We are financing massive government spending (deficits) from printing money to get us through COVID-19. The result? Massive inflation once again!

The Bottom Line

Let's cut to the chase. A combination of bad fiscal policy (federal deficits) and bad monetary policy (printing money) is what causes inflation, and high inflation is a risk to our long-term prosperity. So you may be asking, what can you do as the "voting public" to fix the problems that feel largely out of your reach?

First, understand the nature of inflation and what causes it. Learn how excessive government spending, short-sighted budgeting, and printing money contribute to the instability of sound money and a stable economy.

Then take action. Vote smart. Make yourself heard. *You* must do this— no one else will do it for you. No one else can vote for you. Demand sound government with good economic policies through your voting. Our long-term prosperity is at risk if we continue down the road of huge deficits and printing money, and preserving our long-term prosperity is critical for our kids, grandkids, and all future generations.

Voice your opinions to your representatives. Call for restraints in spending. Ask the government to focus on the critical elements of what the government is meant to do.

The representatives will only follow good policy if the public is behind it. Otherwise, they will continue to be beholden to special interests and cronyism which leads to bad public policy. Their real constituents are, and should always be, the American people. Unfortunately, we the voting public don't have a rich lobby to influence them, but if enough of us let them know what we think, perhaps they will do the right thing.

If they don't get it, then express your opinion at the voting booth in the next election and vote for someone who does.

"*Well, we're going to have to talk about him sometime.*"

CHAPTER 17

Entitlements

While there are many policies about spending that can and should be addressed, I single out entitlements as the eight-hundred-pound gorilla in the room. Why? Because they are the single biggest driver of the federal deficits. Entitlements are the obligations of the government to various constituencies by law for many programs. These are expenditures because of laws passed that created the programs and are now the mandatory spending part of the federal government. These are on "auto-pilot" and are not approved each year as discretionary spending is.

Entitlements are the sole cause of the unfunded obligations relating to Social Security and Medicare. Unfunded obligations represent the promises made for Social Security and Medicare in the future for which there is no revenue to cover. If Social Security and Medicare were self-sustaining, there would be no unfunded obligations. Fixing this problem does not solve all the financial problems, but it is an essential part of the solution. We must understand the issues and deal with this as soon as possible. The longer we wait, the more difficult the solution will be.

The three major programs I'm going to focus on are Social Security (SS)/Disability, Medicare, and Medicaid. Medicare is separated into three parts: Part A is for hospitals; Part B is for medical; and Part D is for drugs. (Medicare C is Medicare Advantage, or MA, which is when private insurance plans are offered through Medicare-approved companies. For the purposes of this book, we don't need to cover this as in depth as the others.) Understanding some of the facts about these programs is crucial before looking at possible solutions.

Social Security and Disability

This program began during the Depression for retirees and the disabled. There was a tax levied on the employee and employer to fund these programs. Over time, a fund was accumulated as income to the program exceeded expenses. People became eligible for receiving full benefits at 65 years old and at 62 years old for reduced benefits. Today, the eligibility is 67 years old for full benefits and still 62 years old for reduced benefits. In the past, there were up to 30 people working for each retiree and the system was financially sound. Today, because of demographic changes, there are 2.6 people working for each retiree. This has resulted in a deficit each year as the income from taxes does not cover the benefits paid out.

The fund will be depleted in 2033, which is less than a decade away. The law provides that when that happens, benefits must be cut so benefits equal income. That will require a 24 percent cut in benefits based on current estimates, rising over time to 26 percent cuts.[1]

Medicare

Part A: Hospital Insurance

Medicare was started in the 1960s to provide medical insurance for those over 65 years old. Part A, hospitalization, is funded by a tax on employees and employers to fund this program. Individuals are eligible for this when they become 65 years old. That age provision has remained. The insurance covers 80 percent of the eligible costs, but an individual can buy private supplemental insurance to cover the rest if they chose to. As a result of demographic changes and rising medical costs, the income from the tax no longer covers the benefits paid.

The fund will be depleted in 2030. The law provides that when that happens, benefits must be cut so that benefits equal income. That will require a 10 percent cut in benefits based on current estimates.[2]

Parts B and D: Medical Insurance and Drug Coverage

These two programs provide optional coverage, for a fee, for medical and drug expenses. Individuals become eligible for this when they become sixty-five years old. There are no taxes or funds to cover this—the only income is from user fees and any shortfall is paid by the general revenues of the government. The user fees cover about 26 percent of the benefits while the other 74 percent comes from the general revenues of the government.[3]

Medicaid

This program was also started in the 1960s to provide medical insurance for low-income people who could not afford insurance. Eligibility for this program is based on income. This is a program that is funded totally by the federal government and the states. There are no user fees. Some percent of the costs are paid by the federal government.

What This Means to You

Figure 17.1 shows a revenue and expense summary of US entitlement programs for the year ending on September 30, 2022:

	Revenue	Expenses	Deficit
Social Security/Disability	$1,135.40	$1218.60	$83.20
Medicare Part A	$382.40	$344.70	($37.70)
Medicare Parts B and D	$161.00	$573.30	$412.30
Medicaid	$0	$654.80	$654.80
Total	$1,678.80	$2,791.40	$1,112.60

*The numbers in this chart are in the billions of dollars.[4]

Figure 17.1. Components of the US's revenue and expenses entitlement program go to funding Social Security and multiple parts of Medicare and Medicaid. Medicaid receives no revenue, but outputs billions, causing a sharp uptick in the totals.

The annual deficit for one year (2022) was $1,112,000,000,000 for just these entitlement programs. This does not include the deficit from the many other entitlement programs.

The unfunded obligations for just Social Security and Medicare (Medicaid is not projected as an unfunded obligation) if we pay benefits as promised under today's law—without the automatic cuts provided by law—will be more than $70 trillion greater than the funds available.[5]

For most people, during your lifetime, the funds for Social Security and Medicare Part A will be depleted. Either benefits will be cut, or if they continue to be paid, there will be significant additional taxes or federal deficits. There are continuing large deficits in Medicare (Parts B and D) and Medicaid which will continue to grow. This is not workable as we are on an unsustainable fiscal path.

There have been many attempts to resolve this and other budget problems. None have succeeded. There are some bills proposed today to help with this, but Congress will not move on any of them. Why? As President Lincoln once said, "With (public sentiment), nothing can fail; against it, nothing can succeed."[6]

To correct these enormous problems, adjustments must be made, and there will be some cost and financial pain to get back to having a self-sustaining program. There is no fairy dust to make it go away. The solutions are difficult financially and politically. But they must be addressed for our long-range survival. If we do not act now, the problem gets postponed until we have no choice and then the financial pain will be much worse. We cannot keep kicking the can down the road giving our children and grandchildren an insoluble problem. We must deal with it now.

In order to deal with the deficit created by entitlements, the public must become more knowledgeable about these programs and the absolute need to fix them while we still can. With understanding, public sentiment will favor action, forcing politicians to address the problem.

It was Winston Churchill who quipped that the American people will always do the right thing—once all other choices are exhausted. We need to do the right thing now, before we run out of choices. We inherited a country that works, and we owe it to future generations to leave them with one that still works. If we continue down the road we are on, we will soon have a country in financial distress.

So how do you eat an eight-hundred-pound gorilla? One bite at a time.

Some Potential Solutions

For many reasons, it's safe to assume that we will not alter the plans for those already receiving benefits or those soon to get them. Given that and looking at this from a ten-thousand-foot aerial view, here are some of the ideas of ways to fix the current programs if we keep on the same structure.

Moving the Age of Eligibility Up

This would be a gradual move and is consistent with the demographic changes which have occurred over time. In fact, a group of US senators is crafting legislation that would raise the Social Security retirement age to seventy. When the programs were started, life expectancy was much lower—today life expectancy is over eighty. The program was not designed for this. How we move it and how quickly will depend on the other changes made.

There is more reason to this solution than our greater life expectancies. Delaying retirement can provide someone with more comfort and ease of living than leaving the workforce can—especially now in the nation's current economic climate, where the barrier for entry for retirement is higher than it has been in the past. Take, for example, Sarah, a substitute teacher in Lincoln, Nebraska. She is sixty-two years old and still working without being in immediate anticipation of retirement. With a steady income, Sarah can continue to live comfortably day-to-day. She trusts that she can cover a dinner out, movie tickets, and other minor indulgences. When her daughter recently came to her, stressed over an unexpected veterinary bill for her cat, Sarah was already prepared to help and was pleased to be able to make things easier for her child. She expends less energy on the mathematics of a saving-and-spending balance that needs to sustain years without income. And, most importantly, she likes her career. Her life is enriched by the work and routine it provides, and she is still in a position where she would miss it if it were to suddenly end. Through continued work, she can meet the standards of her lifestyle and earn enough to keep herself and her close family secure.

Putting away enough money for a lengthy retirement has become quite a feat. If someone can't accomplish it, or if they must work longer than they expected, it doesn't mean that the later stages of their life need to be lacking. Like Sarah—and like our greater life expectancies illustrate—many citizens remain able to work for longer and comfortably access entitlement benefits at later ages. Raising the age of eligibility is an appropriate and practical way to address the debt accumulated by entitlements.

Make It Account-Based

Another approach that would change the structure of how Social Security works is to make it a personal retirement account where each person has his own account and investments. This has been done successfully in other countries and has many advantages. The disadvantage is that there would be a large transition investment required, but that would be less costly over time than the huge unfunded obligations we now face.

For the Medicare side, we could evolve to private health insurance companies handling this instead of the government. This might entail providing government vouchers and letting each party choose their own private insurance company.

Medicare for All

This is a proposed method that, based on our current economic situation, is not recommended. Our goal is to balance the budget—not break the bank. That is what Medicare for all would do if this proposed solution was implemented. The recent proposals would be much more costly than what we are doing now, would have no private insurance, and would have the same problems they have in Canada, Great Britain (which is government-provided health care, not health insurance), and the Scandinavian countries, which do offer private insurance (because it works much better). In all, this does not work well, and we cannot afford it.

—$$$—

There are still more potential solutions:

- **Increase the contributions by individuals and companies for SS and Medicare A.** This would be part of an overall plan to get to self-sustainability. The specific amounts would be part of an overall design by the study commission.
- **Refine the benefits received.** This could mean many things such as limiting the benefits based on income levels or lowering the increases to the benefits paid.
- **Increase the Medicare B and D premiums paid for the insurance.** User fees could be means tested so that higher-income individuals would pay a more realistic premium for the coverage

and lower-income individuals would have smaller increases. In addition, institute a payroll tax to cover some of this cost, as there is no source under the present plan to pay for this other than user fees, which only cover 26 percent of the cost at present.[7]

- **Limit the benefits for various medical procedures based on age or other criteria.**
- **Control the Medicaid cost through block grants to the states which could be phased out over time.** Block grants are specific sums provided to the states for them to provide this insurance.
- **Raise or eliminate the cap on the wages for Social Security.**

The possibilities are endless and need thorough examination by professionals to determine a package that would work practically and politically to make these programs self-sustaining.

These are very complex issues, and the impetus needed to make sustainable solutions will not come from politicians. The public must understand the severity of the problem. Public sentiment for fixing it will come with understanding.

We all need to voice our opinions to our representatives and let them know we want entitlements and uncontrolled spending fixed, with the ultimate goal of moving to a balanced budget as quickly as possible. When public sentiment is behind this, they will feel empowered to fix the problem. Congress needs to appoint a nonpartisan commission to evaluate the programs and find a solution that will make entitlements self-sustaining, focus on what the federal government should be doing, and cut the rest. We cannot have another 2010 Simpson-Bowles Commission event, where months were spent developing excellent recommendations in all areas of government, but few of which were adopted.

It will be impossible to please everyone, and compromises will be needed, but if the result of self-sustainability and a balanced budget is reached with the public supporting the plan, it can be done. No one wants to picture their kids and grandkids waking up one day and asking, "What did our parents and grandparents do to us?" The time to act is now.

Hurry! There's not a second to lose.

CHAPTER 18

What Are We Going to Do?

We have focused on some of the major problems facing our country. To delve into all of them is well beyond the scope of this book—but we have learned something: The current path we are on is disastrous and clearly unsustainable. We should be fearful of continuing to kick the can down the road because we will soon run out of road and go over the proverbial fiscal cliff. The consequences for us, our kids, and grandkids are unimaginable.

It doesn't have to be this way. We can turn this around.

Our history is full of examples of policies that worked well, as well as those that didn't. And experiences from other countries, good and bad, can teach us what to do and what to avoid. Yet we continue to appease some groups with policies that are destructive to everyone and continue to run up the debt to unimaginable levels. No matter how good the "good intentions" may be, bad economic policy is harming us. And if we blow up the whole economy, everyone will be in the disaster together.

So What Do We Know?

Based on empirical evidence and factual data, we know that economies grow fastest when government is limited. Why? Because more capital is left in the productive sector for the entrepreneurs and businesses to use in growing the economy and developing new products. Total increases in output improves the standard of living. By offering products we value at attractive prices, they can make a profit—that is the incentive that makes us grow, and we all benefit as this improves our standard of living. And when businesses succeed and grow, it provides employment and generates funds for more investment. And if they do not offer products or services that we will buy at a profit, they will fail.

The back and forth between businesses and consumers grows the economy. New and better products are produced. Prices drop, making goods and services more affordable to larger and larger groups, including those in lower-income households. Proper incentives explain why.

The best economic systems that drive the highest standard of living for the people in them must have private property and rule of law. People get to keep the fruits of their labor and their property is safe. Individual rights must be protected. Competition will make us all better off by weeding out the bad and rewarding the good as deemed by the ultimate judge and jury—you, us, all of us. A free-market economy is essential, as is government from what we've seen and experienced across multiple countries and throughout time. It has certain functions that it, and only it, can perform. These have been well thought out and enumerated in our Constitution. Using the Constitution to think carefully about government programs that "sound good but feel bad" is a good start.

We know that taxes fund the government, and these must be well-designed to be fair and foster growth. Growth is important so that everyone's lives are improved, especially those living in marginalized communities. But we also know from current experience and historical mistakes that disaster comes from endless spending beyond our means. It is detrimental to our long-term well-being. As noted above, heavy taxation and large debts are not good for growing an economy and excessive spending means large government.

And What Are We to Do?

Something can be done to turn the US fiscal ship around. Let's return the federal government to its essential functions and let states, entrepreneurs, businesses, and people like you and me do the rest.

We have two choices:

1. **Do nothing.** Take the attitude "I am not going to worry about the looming problems because there is nothing I can do."
2. **Take action.** Send a message to our representatives in DC. Demand they "fix this spending and debt problem before we go over the fiscal cliff." If they don't get it and don't start doing the right things, then vote for someone who will do the right thing.

Visit my website at **MainStreetEconomics.org** to learn even more economics and get a good understanding of our problems. Contact your representative using our "Contact Congress" facility on the website to send them a message—ask for action. If you have personal contacts, use them. Call or write. Do anything you can to get this message to your representatives so they can fix this mess.

It is up to us, the folks on Main Street, the "voting public" to decide. We can sit by and watch the destruction wrought by the reckless policies in Washington, or we can take action to get this problem fixed. Only with growing public support can we "move the needle" in Washington, DC, to good economic policy. So don't wait, do it now.

"With (public sentiment), nothing can fail;
without it, nothing can succeed."
—ABRAHAM LINCOLN[1]

"He's been on the phone with our reps ever since he found out
what's really going on with our economy."

Wrapping Things Up

Over the course of this book, we have introduced you to all of the important concepts in basic economics. We've talked about the three key economic systems: free enterprise/market economy (capitalism), socialism, and mixed economic systems (democratic socialism). We have explored the world of microeconomics (how businesses and individuals act) and macroeconomics (how the entire economic system operates). We have explored the role of government in controlling fiscal and monetary policies.

We have also introduced you to some of the most important issues we as a country face, all through a better understanding of basic economics.

Learning economics helps you to understand how our economic system operates and what policies are best for you and the country to achieve a better standard of living for everyone. With this knowledge, you can better understand the most important issues we face and how we can begin to resolve these. You'll be able to better evaluate the proposals from our elected representatives and voice your opinions to them directly or through the voting booth. It is up to you to understand the real implications of policy proposals and look through what the politicians tell you. Sometimes their "pitches" are less than honest in an effort to gain favor with the voters. Well no more.

With this understanding, you can evaluate the policies proposed by different representatives and candidates up for election. Then you can voice your opinions or vote your conscience for whatever you believe is best. The future of our nation depends on it.

Notes

Introduction

1. "Real Time US National Debt Clock | USA Debt Clock.com," n.d. Usadebtclock.com, https://usadebtclock.com/.
2. "Fiscal Data Explains the National Debt," US Treasury Fiscal Data, Accessed September 6, 2023, https://fiscaldata.treasury.gov/americas-finance-guide/national-debt/#:~:text=The%20 inflation%20data%20is%20sourced%20from%20the%20Bureau%20of%20Labor%20 Statistics.&text=Over%20the%20past%20100%20years,to%20%2430.93%20T%20in%20 2022.
3. "Financial Statements of the United States Government for the Fiscal Years Ended September 30, 2022, and 2021," Bureau of Fiscal Service, Accessed August 30, 2023, https://www.fiscal. treasury.gov/files/reports-statements/financial-report/2022/financial-statements-2022.pdf.
4. Molly Dahl et al., "The 2023 Long-Term Budget Outlook," The Congressional Budget Office, Accessed August 30, 2023, https://www.cbo.gov/publication/59331.
5. Statista Research Department, "Forecast of the Gross Federal Debt of the United States for Fiscal Years 2022 to 2033," Statista, February 24, 2023, https://www.statista.com/ statistics/216998/forecast-of-the-federal-debt-of-the-united-states/.

Chapter 2

1. Adam Smith, *An Inquiry into the Nature and Causes of the Wealth of Nations*, (London: Oxford University Press, 2008.)
2. Daniel Ruby, "28 Iphone User Statistics: Sales, Usage & Finances (2023)," *DemandSage*, August 1, 2023, www.demandsage.com/iphone-user-statistics/.
3. Karl Marx and Friedrich Engels, The Communist Manifesto (London: Workers' Education Association, 1848.); Karl Marx, Das Kapital, (Verlag von Otto Meisner, 1867.)
4. Karl Marx, Critique of the Gotha Programme (Moscow: Progress Publishers, 1970.)
5. "Estimated Percent of People of All Ages in Poverty for United States," Federal Reserve Bank of St. Louis, US Census Bureau, Accessed August 30, 2023, https://fred.stlouisfed.org/series/ PPAAUS00000A156NCEN.
6. Marc Schulman, "Poverty in the Sixties," Historycentral.com, 2015, https://www.historycen-tral.com/sixty/Economics/Poverty.html.

Chapter 3:

1. "2022–2023 Confirmations of Highly Pathogenic Avian Influenza in Commercial and Backyard Flocks," USDA APHIS. January 18, 2023, www.aphis.usda.gov/aphis/ourfocus/ animalhealth/animal-disease-information/avian/avian-influenza/hpai-2022/ 2022-hpai-commercial-backyard-flocks.

2. Thomas Sowell, 1993, *Is Reality Optional? and Other Essays*, Hoover Institution Press.

3. Alejandro Gutierrez, "Venezuela and Its Agri-food Crisis: Are We in an Emergency?" Prodavinci, January 11, 2016, https://historico.prodavinci.com/2016/01/11/actualidad/venezuela-y-su-crisis-agroalimentaria-estamos-en-una-emergencia-alimentaria-por-alejandro-gutierrez-s/.

4. "Impacts of Filtering and Rent Control on Housing Supply," HUD User, https://www.huduser.gov/portal/pdredge/pdr-edge-featd-article-061520.html#:~:text=Although%20in%20many%20areas%20filtering%20contributes%20to%20housing,for%20addressing%20the%20shortage%20of%20supply%20are%20high.

Chapter 5:

1. Adam Smith, *An Inquiry into the Nature and Causes of the Wealth of Nations*, (London: Oxford University Press, 2008.)

2. Will Potter, "Bed Bath & Beyond Is Filing for Bankruptcy in DAYS." Mail Online, April 20, 2023, https://www.dailymail.co.uk/news/article-11992541/Bed-Bath-filing-bankruptcy-DAYS-following-tumultuous-years.html.

3. Joseph A. Schumpeter, 1942, *Capitalism, Socialism, and Democracy*, Harper and Brothers.

4. Adam Smith, *An Inquiry into the Nature and Causes of the Wealth of Nations*, (London: Oxford University Press, 2008.)

Chapter 6:

1. Francesco Orilia and Michele Paolini Paoletti, "Properties", *The Stanford Encyclopedia of Philosophy* (Spring 2022 Edition), Edward N. Zalta (ed.), https://plato.stanford.edu/archives/spr2022/entries/properties/.

Chapter 7:

1. "Constitution of the United States: The Preamble," Congress.gov, 2019, https://constitution.congress.gov/constitution/preamble/.

2. Adam Smith, *An Inquiry into the Nature and Causes of the Wealth of Nations*, (London: Oxford University Press, 2008.)

3. Claude Frédéric Bastiat, "That Which Is Seen, and That Which Is Not Seen," Mises Institute, August 18, 2014, https://mises.org/library/which-seen-and-which-not-seen#:~:text=Between%20a%20good%20and%20a%20bad%20economist%20this.

Chapter 8:

1. "The Real Story behind Inflation," n.d. The Heritage Foundation, Accessed August 15, 2023, https://www.heritage.org/budget-and-spending/heritage-explains/the-real-story-behind-inflation.

Chapter 9:

1. Alexis de Tocqueville, "Alexis de Tocqueville," n.d. www.U-S-History.com, Accessed August 17, 2023, https://www.u-s-history.com/pages/h3704.html.

2. Thomas Sowell, "Thomas Sowell Quotes (Author of Basic Economics)," n.d. Goodreads, Accessed August 15, 2023, https://www.goodreads.com/author/quotes/2056.Thomas_Sowell#:~:text=%E2%80%9CWhen%20you%20want%20to%20help%20people%2C%20you%20tell.

3. "Financial Report of the United States Government Fiscal Year 2020," United States Treasury, March 25, 2020, https://www.fiscal.treasury.gov/files/reports-statements/financial-report/2020/fr-03-25-2021-(final).pdf.

4. "Effective Federal Tax Rates," n.d. Www.pgpf.org, Accessed September 1, 2023, https://www.pgpf.org/chart-archive/0102_tax-rates.

5. Christine Bogusz, Dan Ready, and Jorge Salazar, 2021, Review of A Closer Look at Discretionary Spending, Discretionary Spending in Fiscal Year 2020, CBO.gov. April 2021. https://www.cbo.gov/system/files/2021-04/57172-discretionary-spending.pdf.

6. "Annual Deficit or Surplus = Revenues – Outlays," n.d. https://www.cbo.gov/system/files/2021-04/57170-budget-infographic.pdf.

7. Molly Dahl et al., "The 2023 Long-Term Budget Outlook," The Congressional Budget Office, Accessed August 30, 2023, https://www.cbo.gov/publication/59331.

8. Winston Churchill, "Winston Churchill Quotes," n.d. BrainyQuote, https://www.brainyquote.com/quotes/winston_churchill_700209.

9. John Maynard Keynes, 1936, General Theory of Employment, Interest, and Money, Palgrave Macmillan.

10. "EXECUTIVE SUMMARY TO THE 2022 FINANCIAL REPORT OF THE U.S. GOVERNMENT," Bureau of Fiscal Service, Accessed August 30, 2023, https://www.fiscal.treasury.gov/files/reports-statements/financial-report/2022/executive-summary-2022.pdf.

Chapter 11:

1. Historical Census of the Unites States, Colonial Times to 1957, Accessed August 30, 2023, https://www2.census.gov/library/publications/1960/compendia/hist_stats_colonial-1957/hist_stats_colonial-1957-chD.pdf.

Chapter 12:

1. Thomas Jefferson, "Declaration of Independence," National Archives, The U.S. National Archives and Records Administration, July 4, 1776, https://www.archives.gov/founding-docs/declaration-transcript.

2. "Constitution of the United States: The Preamble," Congress.gov, 2019, https://constitution.congress.gov/constitution/preamble/.

3. Adam Smith, *An Inquiry into the Nature and Causes of the Wealth of Nations*, (London: Oxford University Press, 2008.)

Chapter 13:

1. Executive Summary to the FY 2022 Financial Report of the United States Government, Official Website of the United States Government, U.S. Department of the Treasury, 2022, https://www.fiscal.treasury.gov/files/reports-statements/financial-report/2022/executive-summary-2022.pdf.

2. Executive Summary to the FY 2022 Financial Report of the United States Government, Official Website of the United States Government, U.S. Department of the Treasury, 2022, https://www.fiscal.treasury.gov/files/reports-statements/financial-report/2022/executive-summary-2022.pdf.

3. "Financial Statements of the United States Government for the Fiscal Years Ended September 30, 2022, and 2021," Bureau of Fiscal Service, Accessed August 30, 2023, https://www.fiscal.treasury.gov/files/reports-statements/financial-report/2022/financial-statements-2022.pdf.

4. "Financial Statements of the United States Government for the Fiscal Years Ended September 30, 2022, and 2021," Bureau of Fiscal Service, Accessed August 30, 2023, https://www.fiscal.treasury.gov/files/reports-statements/financial-report/2022/financial-statements-2022.pdf.

5. U.S. Department of the Treasury, Fiscal Service, 1966, "Federal Debt: Total Public Debt," FRED, Federal Reserve Bank of St. Louis. January 1, 1966, https://fred.stlouisfed.org/series/GFDEBTN.

Chapter 14:

1. "Electronic Code of Federal Regulations (ECFR)," n.d. Electronic Code of Federal Regulations (ECFR), https://www.ecfr.gov/.
2. Patrick McLaughlin, Nita Ghei, and Michael Wilt, "Regulatory Accumulation and Its Costs," Mercatus Center, November 14, 2018, https://www.mercatus.org/research/policy-briefs/regulatory-accumulation-and-its-costs-0#:~:text=Research%20by%20the%20Mercatus%20Center%20at%20George%20Mason,2012%20%28had%20regulations%20stayed%20at%201980%20levels%29.%20.
3. Lindsay Cates, 2022, "4 Small Business Owners Explain What They Need from Government to Navigate Uncertainty," www.uschamber.com, June 16, 2022, https://www.uschamber.com/small-business/3-small-business-owners-explain-what-they-need-from-government-to-navigate-uncertainty.
4. Bentley Coffey, Patrick A. McLaughlin, and Pietro Peretto, 2020, "The Cumulative Cost of Regulations," Review of Economic Dynamics, April, https://doi.org/10.1016/j.red.2020.03.004.
5. Steve Eder, 2017, "When Picking Apples on a Farm with 5,000 Rules, Watch out for the Ladders," The New York Times, December 27, 2017, sec. Business, https://www.nytimes.com/2017/12/27/business/picking-apples-on-a-farm-with-5000-rules-watch-out-for-the-ladders.html.

Chapter 15:

1. BBC News, 2021, "John Kerry: UK Climate Summit Is World's 'Last Best Chance,'" January 28, 2021, sec. US & Canada, https://www.bbc.com/news/world-us-canada-55836163.
2. "Electric Power Sector CO2 Emissions Drop as Generation Mix Shifts from Coal to Natural Gas," n.d. Www.eia.gov, Accessed August 15, 2023, https://www.eia.gov/todayinenergy/detail.php?id=48296#:~:text=Lower%20CO%202%20emissions%20have%20largely%20been%20a.
3. "Nuclear," U.S. Department of Energy, Accessed August 30, 2023, https://www.energy.gov/nuclear.
4. Hannah Ritchie, "What Are the Safest and Cleanest Sources of Energy?" Our World in Data, February 10, 2020, https://ourworldindata.org/safest-sources-of-energy#:~:text=The%20key%20insight%20is%20that.
5. "Information Library - World Nuclear Association," n.d. Www.world-Nuclear.org, Accessed September 15, 2023, https://www.world-nuclear.org/information-library/index.aspx.
6. "Revenue of the Electricity Industry in the United States from 1970 to 2021," Statista, Accessed August 30, 2023, https://www.statista.com/statistics/190548/revenue-of-the-us-electric-power-industry-since-1970/.
7. "U.S. Energy Facts Explained," U.S. Energy Information Administration, June 12, 2023, https://www.eia.gov/energyexplained/us-energy-facts/.

Chapter 16:

1. Justinas Baltrusaitis, "'Real Value' of One U.S. Dollar Decreases by 86% in the Last 50 Years," Finbold, March 21, 2022, https://finbold.com/real-value-of-one-u-s-dollar-decreases-by-86-in-the-last-50-years/.

2. "Hussman Funds - Weekly Market Comment: Inflation Myth and Reality - January 19, 2010," n.d. Www.hussmanfunds.com, Accessed September 1, 2023, http://www.hussmanfunds.com/wmc/wmc100119.htm.
3. "Inflation, Consumer Prices for the United States," Federal Reserve Bank of St. Louis, Accessed August 30, 2023, https://fred.stlouisfed.org/series/FPCPITOTLZGUSA.
4. "Inflation, Consumer Prices for the United States," Federal Reserve Bank of St. Louis, Accessed August 30, 2023, https://fred.stlouisfed.org/series/FPCPITOTLZGUSA.

Chapter 17:

1. Scott Horsley, "Social Security is now expected to run short of cash by 2023," National Public Radio, March 31, 2023, https://www.npr.org/2023/03/31/1167378958/social-security-medicare-entitlement-programs-budget.2.
2. "A SUMMARY OF THE 2023 ANNUAL REPORTS," Social Security Administration, Accessed August 30, 2023, https://www.ssa.gov/OACT/TRSUM/index.html#:~:text=The%20Trustees%20of%20the%20Social%20Security%20and%20Medicare,programs%20both%20continue%20to%20face%20significant%20financing%20issues.
3. "A SUMMARY OF THE 2023 ANNUAL REPORTS," Social Security Administration, Accessed August 30, 2023, https://www.ssa.gov/OACT/TRSUM/index.html#:~:text=The%20Trustees%20of%20the%20Social%20Security%20and%20Medicare,programs%20both%20continue%20to%20face%20significant%20financing%20issues.
4. "A SUMMARY OF THE 2023 ANNUAL REPORTS," Social Security Administration, Accessed August 30, 2023, https://www.ssa.gov/OACT/TRSUM/index.html#:~:text=The%20Trustees%20of%20the%20Social%20Security%20and%20Medicare,programs%20both%20continue%20to%20face%20significant%20financing%20issues.
5. "Financial Report of the United States Government - Management," n.d. Fiscal.treasury.gov, Accessed September 1, 2023, https://fiscal.treasury.gov/reports-statements/financial-report/mda-unsustainable-fiscal-path.html.
6. Abraham Lincoln, "Abraham Lincoln Quote," n.d. Lib Quotes, Accessed August 15, 2023, https://libquotes.com/abraham-lincoln/quote/lbr7o1w.
7. "A SUMMARY OF THE 2023 ANNUAL REPORTS," Social Security Administration, Accessed August 30, 2023, https://www.ssa.gov/OACT/TRSUM/index.html#:~:text=The%20Trustees%20of%20the%20Social20Security%20and%20Medicare,programs%20both%20continue%20to%20face%20significant%20financing%20issues.

Chapter 18:

1. Abraham Lincoln, "Abraham Lincoln Quote," n.d. Lib Quotes, Accessed August 15, 2023, https://libquotes.com/abraham-lincoln/quote/lbr7o1w.

Illustration Credits

Chapter 3

Figure 3.1. Source: Data from Ashish Kumar Srivastav, Law of Demand, Wall Street Mojo, https://www.wallstreetmojo.com/law-of-demand/.

Figure 3.3. Source: Data from Sybil Evans, The Law of Supply, SidePlayer, last modified 2015, https://slideplayer.com/slide/6274126/.

Chapter 8

Figure 8.3. Data from U.S. Bureau of Economic Analysis, Real gross domestic product per capita [A939RX0Q048SBEA] (FRED, Federal Reserve Bank of St. Louis, 2023). https://fred.stlouisfed.org/series/A939RX0Q048SBEA.

Figure 8.4. Data from U.S. Bureau of Labor Statistics, Unemployment Rate (FRED, Federal Reserve Bank of St. Louis, 2023). https://fred.stlouisfed.org/graph/?g=1b5t0.

Chapter 9

Figure 9.1. Data from Congressional Budget Office, An Update to the Budget Outlook: 2023 to 2033, May 2023. Image credit: The U.S. tax system is progressive, with higher-income taxpayers facing higher tax rates (Peter G. Peterson Foundation, 2023). https://www.pgpf.org/finding-solutions/understanding-the-budget/revenues.

Figure 9.4. Data from Congressional Budget Office, The 2023 Long-Term Budget Outlook, June 2023, and Office of Management and Budget, Historical Tables, Budget of the Unites States Government: Fiscal Year 2024, March 2023. Image credit: The growing debt is caused by a structural mismatch between spending and revenues (Peter G. Peterson Foundation, 2023). https://www.pgpf.org/blog/2023/07/the-national-debt-could-nearly-double-in-size-over-the-next-30-years#:~:text=The%20mismatch%20between%20revenues%20and,between%20federal%20receipts%20and%20outlays.

Figure 9.5. Data from Congressional Budget Office, The Budget and Economic Outlook: 2023 to 2033, February 2023. Image credit: Spending for Mandatory programs and interest is projected to outpace all other non-interest spending (Peter G. Peterson Foundation, 2023). https://www.pgpf.org/blog/2023/07/the-national-debt-could-nearly-double-in-size-over-the-next-30-years#:~:text=The%20mismatch%20between%20revenues%20and,between%20federal%20receipts%20and%20outlays.

Chapter 10

Figure 10.2. Data from Board of Governors of the Federal Reserve System (US), Monetary Base; Total [BOGMBASE] (FRED, Federal Reserve Bank of St. Louis, 2023). https://fred.stlouisfed.org/graph/?g=1b5t4.

Chapter 13

Figure 13.2. Data from U.S. Department of the Treasury, Fiscal Service, Federal Debt: Total Public Debt [GFDEBTN] (FRED, Federal Reserve Bank of St. Louis, 2023). https://fred.stlouisfed.org/graph/?g=1b5t6.

Figure 13.3. Data from U.S. Office of Management and Budget and Federal Reserve Bank of St. Louis, Federal Debt: Total Public Debt as Percent of Gross Domestic Product [GFDEGDQ188S] (FRED, Federal Reserve Bank of St. Louis, 2023). https://fred.stlouisfed.org/graph/?g=1b5t7.

Chapter 16

Figure 16.1. Data from U.S. Bureau of Labor Statistics, Consumer Price Index for All Urban Consumers: All Items in U.S. City Average [CPIAUCSL] (FRED, Federal Reserve Bank of St. Louis, 2023). https://fred.stlouisfed.org/graph/?g=1bpcK.

About the Author

Leslie A. Rubin is a professional accountant, entrepreneur, philanthropist, and real estate developer. He has studied economics for over forty years and has been heavily involved with economic education locally, working with schools, writing articles, and commissioning sculptures on economic themes for his real estate developments, which allowed him to gain a clear understanding of what makes economic systems work and the power of incentives. Rubin's passion for economics and economic education inspired him to create Main Street Economics Inc., a nonpartisan, nonprofit organization that provides the average person on "Main Street" the opportunity to learn about economic systems without going back to school.

Les graduated from University of North Carolina at Chapel Hill in accounting and was elected to Phi Beta Kappa and Beta Gamma Sigma honor societies. For ten years he was a practicing CPA/controller and has been the owner and president of his own commercial real estate development company, RRR Realty Services, for almost fifty years.